Other Titles in the New Glucose Revolution Series

For the definitive overview of the glycemic index...
* *The New Glucose Revolution (third edition): The Authoritative Guide to the Glycemic Index—the Dietary Solution for Lifelong Health*

For a focus on recipes, shopping, and the GI in the larger nutrition picture...
* *The New Glucose Revolution Low GI Vegetarian Cookbook*
* *The New Glucose Revolution Low GI Family Cookbook*
* *The New Glucose Revolution Life Plan*
* *The New Glucose Revolution Shopper's Guide to GI Values 2008*
* *The New Glucose Revolution Low GI Guide to Sugar and Energy*

For a basic introduction to the GI plus the top 100 low GI foods...
* *The New Glucose Revolution Low GI Eating Made Easy: The Beginner's Guide to Eating with the Glycemic Index*

For a focus on weight-loss...
* *The Low GI Diet Revolution: The Definitive Science-Based Weight Loss Plan*
* *The Low GI Diet Cookbook: 100 Simple, Delicious Smart-Carb Recipes—The Proven Way to Lose Weight and Eat for Lifelong Health*
* *The New Glucose Revolution Low GI Guide to Losing Weight*

For a focus on the GI and specific health conditions...
* *The New Glucose Revolution for Diabetes: The Definitive Guide to Managing Diabetes and Prediabetes Using the Glycemic Index*
* *The New Glucose Revolution Low GI Gluten-Free Eating Made Easy: The Essential Guide to the Glycemic Index and Gluten-Free Living*
* *The New Glucose Revolution Low GI Guide to the Metabolic Syndrome and Your Heart: The Only Authoritative Guide to Using the Glycemic Index for Better Heart Health*
* *The New Glucose Revolution What Makes My Blood Glucose Go Up . . . And Down?: 101 Frequently Asked Questions about Your Blood Glucose Level*
* *The New Glucose Revolution Guide to Living Well with PCOS*

To stay up to date with the latest research on carbohydrates, the GI and your health, and the latest books in the series, check out the free online monthly newsletter *GI News*, produced by Dr. Jennie Brand-Miller's GI Group at the University of Sydney: http://ginews.blogspot.com

Low GI
family cookbook

Dr. Jennie Brand-Miller

Kaye Foster-Powell

Anneka Manning

Philippa Sandall

Da Capo

LIFE LONG

A Member of the
Perseus Books Group

contents

foreword   vi
introduction   vii

part one—food is a family affair   1
menu plans for children   41

part two—recipes with a healthy balance   51
breakfasts and brunches   55
snacks   73
lunch   93
main dishes   111
desserts and sweet treats   149
basics   165

pantry revamp   175
directory   179
acknowledgments   180
index   181

Foreword

The importance of childhood nutrition has gained a great deal of recognition over recent years and many families are now discovering what scientists and nutritionists have known for decades: good food is an essential component of child health in many different ways.

A nutritious diet provides your child with good eating habits for life, strong teeth and bones, healthy skin, a healthy weight and improved behavior. The benefits of childhood nutrition are enormous, but getting children to actually eat healthy foods is another challenge altogether, as we parents know only too well!

In this delightful book, the authors (all incredibly well qualified and highly regarded as nutrition professionals—and mothers) show us how quick and easy it can be to place nutritious and delicious foods in front of our children— food that they will not be able to resist.

This beautifully illustrated book is exactly what busy parents need to fulfill our duties as gatekeepers of our children's health and as the family food supply, creative chefs and child psychologists. It is such a challenge to come up with interesting, nutritious foods every day, and it is even more challenging to think of new food ideas, recipes that work and ways of engaging children in healthy food preparation and cooking.

I applaud this comprehensive and very timely compilation of sound new nutrition information, practical nutritious cooking and beautifully presented recipe ideas in a book that every family can benefit from.

Dr. Jenny O'Dea
Associate Professor in Nutrition & Health Education
Faculty of Education & Social Work
The University of Sydney

Introduction

Feeding our children presents challenges as well as rewards. From our own experience, we know what a pleasure it is to see our children enjoy the meals we have prepared. We also know about the other times—when they dash out the door without eating breakfast, refuse to try new foods, fuss if the bread is brown, or push the vegetables around the plate.

Children need our guidance to learn how to respect their health and look after their bodies. Helping them develop good eating habits is part of this. As parents we often need a helping hand, too. And that's why we wrote this book.

It's about parents and children cooking together, eating together and developing healthy eating habits for life. We show you what eating foods with a low glycemic index (GI) is about and how you can expand your family's choices to incorporate these healthy carbohydrates.

Many of the recipes are our own favorites. We hope you and your children enjoy them and that they give you all a love of good food—for life.

Kaye, Anneka, Jennie and Philippa

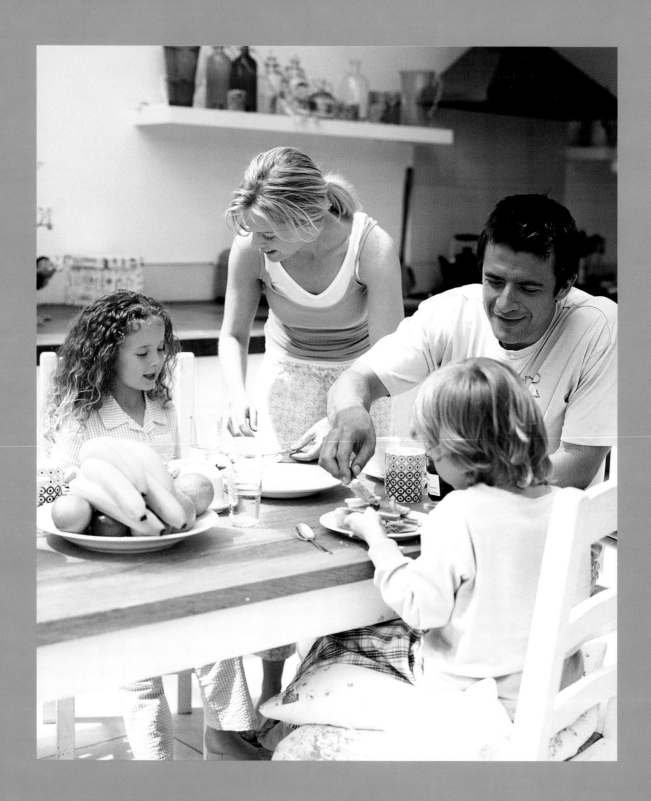

part one

food is a family affair

Raising food-smart kids

We shape our children's health and well-being from the moment they are conceived. What a woman eats when she is pregnant influences her baby's health in many ways. The nourishment her baby receives in the womb shapes how its body grows. The flavors of foods she eats can play a part in her child's later food preferences, and her baby's birth weight can predict the risk of chronic conditions such as obesity, diabetes and heart disease later in life.

As children grow, the food we give them continues to be important, but *how* we do it also matters. Our own eating habits—whether we sit down to family meals, grab food on the run or watch television while we eat—will influence how our children behave. The way we treat food will also play a part in their feelings about food and their bodies.

Here are some practical tips for raising food-smart kids:

* be a role model: eat the foods you would like your children to eat
* have regular family meals
* offer a range of foods of high nutritional quality at meals and snack times. Children have higher nutrient requirements from a smaller quantity of food than adults, so it is important that the foods they do eat are nutrient-dense
* involve kids in the process of food choice and preparation, and
* keep mealtimes happy; do your utmost to avoid battles over food.

No one has said it more clearly and simply than American nutritionist Ellyn Satter: "As parents we have the responsibility of choosing when, where and what is available to our children to eat. Our children have the responsibility of choosing how much and even whether they eat."

Everyday healthy eating guidelines

It is our hope that this book will help to answer some of those 101 questions parents ask. Following the tips below will go a long way to encouraging healthy eating habits:

* aim for 2 servings of fruit and 5 servings of vegetables
* include whole-grain breads and cereals with a low GI
* choose reduced fat dairy products or calcium-enriched alternatives for children over 2 years of age
* include protein from a variety of sources, including: lean red meats, poultry, eggs, fish, seafood and legumes (such as baked beans, chickpeas, lentils and kidney beans)
* incorporate sources of monounsaturated and omega-3 polyunsaturated fats such as olive and canola oils, nuts, seeds, oily fish and avocado
* balance food intake with physical activity, and
* keep foods that are high in salt, added fat or added sugar for occasional treats rather than everyday foods.

We don't have any health problems. Why do we need to eat a low GI diet?

We are often asked about low GI eating and why it matters if you are healthy anyway. One reason is simply to feel even better! Low GI eating has advantages for everyone—including healthy, growing children. That's because low GI foods:

* are more filling
* help reduce hunger between meals and therefore lessen the likelihood of overeating
* promote healthy blood fats
* stabilize blood glucose levels which can help with energy levels
* reduce the risk of obesity
* can lessen the symptoms and severity of acne, and
* reduce the risk of type 2 diabetes.

In a nutshell, low GI eating means that you are eating foods closer to the way nature intended and that your body is doing most (or all) of the processing, not the food manufacturer. It also fits with the first dietary guideline of all countries around the world: "Eat a wide variety of foods." And it's easy because low GI foods can be found in four of the five food groups:

* whole kernel grains and pasta in the bread and cereals group
* milk and yogurt among the dairy foods
* legumes of all types in the meat and alternatives group, and
* virtually all fruits and vegetables.

What is the GI?

Carbohydrates are one of the best sources of energy for our bodies, benefiting our brains and muscles. Most people don't eat too much carbohydrate. But most people *do* eat the wrong kind of carbohydrate because not all carbohydrates are created equal. This is where the GI comes in. It's about recognizing any "smart carbs"—the low GI ones—and making sure we include them in our meals and snacks.

The GI (glycemic index) helps us tell the difference between the various carbohydrate foods we eat and how our bodies use them.

- Carbohydrates with a low GI (55 or less) will make your blood glucose rise slowly and fall gently over a longer time.

- Carbohydrates with a high GI (70 or more) are the ones your body will digest quickly causing your blood glucose levels to surge and then crash, rather like being on a roller-coaster ride.

Research has shown that most of us eat too many high GI foods and not enough low ones, putting us at risk of developing significant health problems.

 When shopping, look out for the international GI symbol.

For more information on the GI, visit: www.glycemicindex.com or subscribe (free) to *GI News:* http://ginews.blogspot.com

We like to say that low GI eating is for everybody, every day, every meal.

What do children need to eat?

The seemingly vast amounts of energy that children appear to use up in running around can be met with surprisingly small amounts of food. The catch is that these little bits of food need to be rich in nutrients. So exactly what does this mean?

Compare a couple of plain sweet cookies with a slice of whole-grain or mixed grain bread. Both provide about the same amount of calories, carbohydrate, protein and fat. The difference lies in the little things: the bread contains at least twice as much iron, zinc, calcium and magnesium, and five times more fiber than the cookies.

Naturally, children differ, and exactly how much food each child needs for good health depends on their age, gender and activity levels. Some days children will seem to eat loads and other days next to nothing. Growth spurts and puberty usually trigger increases in intake. The recommended amounts that follow are simply an average guide to the minimum daily intake your child should be receiving.

Making mealtimes happier

Compared to television, computer games, toys, riding bikes, skateboarding or playing with friends, sitting down to eat dinner with the family does not rank highly on the fun scale. So don't be hard on yourself. Cheer the meal along with some of these ideas.

* Make mealtime a regular event at a regular time.
* Clear toys, books and other distractions from the table.
* Turn off the television, computer and mobile phone.
* Involve children in cooking the meal and setting the table.
* Give them some choice, for example, water or milk to drink, canteloupe or banana for dessert.
* Don't force kids to finish their meals, but insist on a taste of everything.
* Teach littlies to count. You could line up carrot rings, green beans and baby potatoes. Have them add them up and then work out how many are left as they eat them.
* If they're only halfway through the meal and already looking like they need to wriggle out of their seat, a race to finish can work as a challenge to reignite interest in eating. Don't use it every day, but on the odd occasion it works like a dream between siblings.

Fruit and vegetables

Of all the foods we eat, fruit and vegetables are the most important source of vitamin C, which helps fight infections, heal wounds and keep our gums, teeth and bones strong and healthy. Our bodies also use it to make collagen, the protein that gives our skin strength and elasticity. Fruit and vegetables are also an essential source of folate, especially citrus fruit like oranges and mandarins, leafy green vegetables, green peas and legumes (dried beans and peas). Our children need folate for normal growth. Not having enough can cause a range of subtle symptoms—such as irritability, forgetfulness and digestive disorders. Pregnant women need folate to help prevent neural tube defects and promote a good birth weight for their baby.

Fruit and vegetables also provide something few of us get enough of: dietary fiber, for healthy hearts, healthy bowels and, of course, to keep us regular. Filling, high-fiber foods can also help us stick to a healthy weight by reducing hunger pangs. (See page 15 for more about fiber.)

Choose a rainbow

Goodness comes from variety, so choose a rainbow of colors, knowing that each fruit and vegetable has a unique complement of vitamins, minerals, fiber and disease-prevention benefits.

Fresh, frozen or canned—what's best?

Think fresh fruit and vegetables are always the most nutritious? Think again. If you can't grow your own produce and eat it within hours of harvesting, canned and frozen fruits and vegetables can be every bit as good for you as fresh ones, and in some cases even better. What matters is that you and your family eat more fruits and vegetables, whether they be fresh, frozen or canned— whatever best fits your lifestyle and your budget.

Fruit

How much each day?

AGE RANGE	RECOMMENDED MINIMUM (AVERAGE)
2–3 years	1 serving
4–8 years	1–2 servings
9–13 years	2–3 servings
14–18 years	2–4 servings

One serving is equivalent to:

* 1 small- to medium-sized piece fresh fruit such as an apple, banana, mango, orange, peach or pear (about $4^1/_4$–$5^1/_4$oz)
* 2 small pieces fresh fruit such as apricots, kiwifruit or plums (about $2^1/_4$oz each)
* 1 cup fresh small fruit, or diced or canned fruit pieces, including grapes, fruit salad, berries and sliced peaches
* 4–5 dried apricot halves, apple rings, dates, figs or prunes (about 1oz)
* 1–2 tablespoons raisins or currants
* $^1/_2$–$^3/_4$ cup fruit juice, homemade, or unsweetened, 100 percent juice.

How can I get my toddler to eat fresh fruit?

If there are other options available that they prefer, you can't really blame them. Try limiting those options by cutting up two or three different types of fruit and putting a small selection on a plate. Put this in front of your child when you know it's been a few hours since they've eaten and leave them with it. Don't pressure them to eat it, and ignore any protests or requests for something different. Ensure no other food is available until the next mealtime.

Vegetables

When we asked our friends what sorts of answers they would like to find in a book on feeding children, the universal request was tips to get them to eat their greens (and any other colored vegetable, for that matter).

* Think finger food and make it easy to eat: carrot and celery sticks, slices of bell pepper, broccoli or cauliflower florets, beans, snow peas and corn kernels.
* Think small, easy bites (and not just for the littlies). Baby carrots and tiny tomatoes appeal to children of all ages and stages. Keep them handy and ready to eat.
* Think raw rather than cooked. Some people just prefer to crunch. So if it's hard to get the family to eat cooked carrots, cabbage or broccoli, raw may be the answer. Make sure you wash it well first.
* Think this-goes-with-that. Make a feast for the eyes and add color to soups and stews with peas, sweet corn, carrots, peppers, celery and spring (green) onions, or stir-fry them with noodles, or make a pilaf or fried rice dish, or toss them through a pasta salad. Bright and beautiful is very tempting.
* Think now-you-see-me-now-you-don't. Fruit and vegetables don't have to be seen to do their job. Puree them in soups, or grate and add them to breads, muffins and burgers.
* Think "do what I do" not just "what I say" and pile your own plate high with vegetables.

Cooking tips for vegetables

* Leave skins on whenever you can or peel very thinly.
* Avoid soaking vegetables in water before cooking them.
* Use a steamer or microwave to retain the most nutrients.
* Cook vegetables such as carrots or potatoes in big chunks to retain nutrients.
* Reduce the amount of water you use for cooking, cover the pan and cook quickly and as close to serving time as possible. Never add baking soda or salt to the cooking water.
* Cook vegetables until they are softened but still firm to the bite.

How much each day?

AGE RANGE	RECOMMENDED MINIMUM (AVERAGE)
2–3 years	2 servings
4–8 years	3 servings
9–13 years	4–5 servings
14–18 years	5–6 servings

One serving is equivalent to:
* $\frac{1}{2}$ cup cooked vegetables such as carrot, pumpkin, corn, potato, peas, chopped green beans, broccoli or cauliflower
* $\frac{1}{2}$ cup mashed potato
* 1 cup raw, leafy vegetables such as lettuce, cabbage or spinach
* 1 cup vegetable soup (without cream!)
* 1 cup pure vegetable juice

How can I get my kids to eat green things?

You may know that two to three servings of vegetables is the aim of the game for young children, but how do you ensure they get the message? Children won't eat something just because it's good for them. It has to look good, taste good, smell good and feel good! So offer vegetables in all sorts of ways: baked, juiced, mashed, stir-fried, steamed, raw, grated, under cheese sauce, in soups and with dips.

And don't leave vegetables until the end of the day. Young children can be tired and fragile by dinnertime so getting them to eat all their dinner, let alone their vegetables, is a big ask. Try to incorporate vegetables as a normal part of eating throughout the day, or while they're feeling hungry waiting for dinner, give them a bowl of carrot sticks to munch through.

Breads and cereals with a low GI

Carbohydrate-rich breads and cereals (rice, wheat, oats, barley and rye, and products made from them such as bread, pasta and breakfast cereals) provide a lot more than just energy. They are one of the major sources of B-group vitamins and, in whole-grain and fortified forms, make a significant contribution to our intake of minerals including magnesium and iron—they can provide at least half a child's iron needs. And if you choose the low GI ones, they'll keep you and your family feeling fuller for longer.

These days, supermarket shelves are packed with high GI flours and grains. Breakfast cereals are a good example. Once, a bowl of slowly digested porridge made with traditional rolled oats gave most of us the energy to keep going from breakfast through to lunchtime. Nowadays we are more likely to fill that breakfast bowl with high GI crunchy flakes that will spike our blood glucose and insulin levels and leave us needing a mid-morning snack to keep going. A simple swap is all it takes to reduce the GI of your diet. To get started, replace some of those high GI breads and breakfast cereals with low GI carbs that will trickle fuel into your engine. Our recipes will show you how.

What about doughnuts, cookies, crackers and cakes?

Although related to breads and cereals (because they are made from flour), these foods aren't suitable as regular substitutes. They provide carbohydrate but very few nutrients. Feeding children these foods is a bit like growing plants with water but no fertilizer: it keeps them alive but they certainly won't flourish. Instead, these are treats or indulgences to be included occasionally. Eating them regularly will mean your child's intake of saturated fat and salt is excessive.

How much each day?

AGE RANGE	RECOMMENDED MINIMUM (AVERAGE)
2–3 years	3 servings
4–8 years	4–5 servings
9–13 years	5–6 servings
14–18 years	6–7 servings

One serving is equivalent to:
* 1 slice (1oz) bread (sandwich thickness)
* half an English muffin or bagel
* $\frac{1}{2}$ cup breakfast cereal, rolled oats or muesli
* $\frac{1}{2}$ cup (the size of a tennis ball) cooked rice or other small grains (such as bulgur or couscous) or cooked pasta or noodles

What you need to know about filling, high-fiber foods

There are two types of fiber, soluble and insoluble, and we need both. Dietary fiber *only* comes from plant foods—it is found in the outer bran layers of grains (corn, oats, wheat and rice, and in foods containing these grains), fruit, vegetables, nuts and legumes (dried beans, peas and lentils).

* *Soluble fibers* are the gel, gum and often jelly-like part of apples, pears, strawberries, blueberries and other fruits, traditional porridge oats and legumes.
* *Insoluble fibers* are dry and bran-like—think roughage. All cereal grains and products that retain the outer coat of the grain they are made from are sources, along with whole-grain foods, whole-wheat breads, barley, brown rice, bulgur, wheat bran and seeds.

Meat, poultry, fish, seafood, eggs and legumes

Primarily recognized as a source of protein, this food group helps us meet our iron, zinc and B vitamin requirements. Variety is the key: include lean red meat about three times a week, eggs or skinless chicken once or twice a week, and fish or other seafood at least once or twice a week. Try to include legumes (beans) at least twice a week, and even more often if you or your children are vegetarian. Just $1/2$ cup of cooked lentils contains almost 5mg of iron, which is half the recommended daily intake for children aged 4–8 years.

The special benefits of fish

Fish has a type of polyunsaturated fat known as omega-3. This "good fat" is believed to lower the risk of heart disease in adults and has also been found to improve brain development in babies. For this reason, pregnant and breast-feeding women are encouraged to eat fish and seafood regularly.

Oily fish are the richest source of omega-3 fats. One of the most convenient sources for children is canned salmon, but fresh fish with higher levels of omega-3s include Atlantic salmon, sea mullet, southern bluefin tuna, swordfish, and Atlantic, Pacific and Spanish mackerel. Eastern and Pacific oysters and squid (calamari) are also rich sources.

Canned pink and red salmon (including the bones), sardines, mackerel and, to a lesser extent, tuna, are all rich sources of omega-3s. Look for canned fish packed in water, canola oil, olive oil or tomato sauce, and drain well.

Mercury in fish

The Food and Drug Administration recommends limiting consumption of some types of fish that may contain higher levels of mercury, a toxic heavy metal. The strictest precautions apply to pregnant women, women planning pregnancy and children. For more information, go to www.cfsan.fda.gov/~dms/admehg3.html

How much each day?

AGE RANGE	RECOMMENDED MINIMUM (AVERAGE)
2–3 years	1–2 half servings
4–8 years	1–2 half servings
9–13 years	1–2 servings
14–18 years	1–2 servings

One serving is equivalent to:

* $3^1/2$oz raw lean meat or chicken (this is the size of a deck of cards)
* 2 medium eggs
* $1/2$ cup cooked lean ground meat
* $1/2$ small skinless chicken breast
* 1 large chicken drumstick
* $5^1/2$oz raw fish or seafood
* 4oz grilled or steamed fish
* $3^1/2$oz canned fish (drained)
* 1 cup cooked beans, lentils, chickpeas or whole dried or split peas

My child won't eat meat—what should I do?

Not all children are the same, but some are just plain lazy when it comes to chewing food and this can manifest as a refusal to eat meat.

Obviously the main nutrient they're missing by not eating meat is iron. Tuna, salmon, chicken and eggs don't usually provoke the same obstinacy (or chewing challenge) as red meat and they are also good sources of iron, so don't hesitate to use them as options as well. Try not to always resort to sausages, and take a leaf out of the book of vegetarians and incorporate more legumes (baked beans, chickpeas, hummus, tofu) and other sources of iron such as dried apricots, dried peaches, and iron-fortified and whole-grain cereals and breads. Including a source of vitamin C, like some fruit or raw vegetables, with these foods will enhance absorption of the iron.

Dairy foods

The key to strong healthy bones is to make sure you and your family have plenty of calcium in your diet. That's why dairy foods are recommended throughout childhood and beyond. Not only are they an important source of calcium but they also provide energy, protein, carbohydrate and vitamins A, B and D. And virtually all dairy foods have low GI values—largely thanks to lactose, the sugar found naturally in milk, which has a low GI of 46. Because the number of children who are overweight is increasing, reduced fat dairy foods are recommended from 2 years of age.

Boning up on non-dairy calcium sources

If you eat only plant foods or want to avoid dairy products, calcium-fortified soy products may be for you. Other non-dairy options that will boost your calcium intake include almonds, brazil nuts, sesame seeds, dried figs, dried apricots, soybeans, dark leafy greens, dried legumes, Asian greens such as bok choy, calcium-enriched tofu and calcium-fortified breakfast cereals.

My daughter refuses to drink milk. What should I do?

A couple of servings of dairy are recommended each day to meet calcium requirements. Sometimes a little tempter like a fun cup or special straw is all that's needed. Otherwise, you could try a spoonful of flavoring. Alternative dairy foods such as yogurt, cheese, custard, icecream or a dairy dessert are all great sources of calcium, too. As another option, try a reduced fat, calcium-enriched soy drink.

How much each day?

AGE RANGE	RECOMMENDED MINIMUM (AVERAGE)
2–3 years	2 servings
4–8 years	2 servings
9–13 years	3 servings
14–18 years	3 servings

One serving is equivalent to:
* 1 cup milk—choose fat free, skim or low fat milk most often (for children over 2)
* 1 cup calcium-enriched soy milk
* 1 cup low fat yogurt or calcium-enriched soy yogurt
* 1$\frac{1}{2}$oz hard cheese—use reduced fat varieties most often
* $\frac{1}{3}$ cup shredded cheese—use reduced fat varieties most often
* $\frac{1}{2}$ cup skim or reduced fat evaporated milk.

Once children are weaned, too much milk (more than 2 cups a day) can hinder iron absorption and contribute to an inadequate iron intake.

Fats and oils

Children need fat for energy, growth, brain development and a healthy immune system, but too much fat, particularly of the wrong type, can pave the way for obesity, heart disease and diabetes.

For babies, breastmilk and infant formula are high in fat to sustain the rapid growth that occurs during the first year of life. Once weaned, children start obtaining fat from other foods and between 2 and 3 years of age growth slows down and fat becomes less important in the diet. As children begin consuming a more varied diet, the type of fat in their diet should become a higher consideration. Saturated fats carry many health risks and total fat intake needs to be moderated.

Tips for limiting saturated fats

* Minimize the use of butter and use monounsaturated and polyunsaturated margarines instead. Go easy on the amount you spread and leave it out completely when you're using a higher fat topping such as peanut butter, cheese spread, cheese, chocolate-hazelnut spread, avocado or mayonnaise.
* Use small amounts of a range of different oils in food preparation. For example, canola for general frying, olive for salad dressing and sesame for an Asian stir-fry.
* Trim the fat from meat and remove the skin from chicken.
* Limit higher fat meats such as sausages, bacon, beef, chicken loaf or chicken nuggets to no more than once a week.
* Choose low fat dairy products, especially ice cream, custard, yogurt and cheese.
* Incorporate fish, seafood and omega-3 eggs to boost polyunsaturated omega-3 intake.
* Be selective if you eat out regularly and help children to look for alternatives to fried dishes and creamy, cheesy or buttery sauces or toppings.
* Read labels when buying cookies, cakes, muesli bars and other packet snacks. If the saturated fat content is more than 20 percent of the total fat, put it back on the shelf.

How much fat do kids need?

A reasonable amount of fat for a child is around 30 percent of their daily calorie intake. For 4–8 year olds this equates to $1^3/_4$–$2^1/_4$oz, for older kids around $2^1/_4$–$2^3/_4$oz of fat per day. Much of this fat will come from meats and alternatives, cereal, dairy foods and from the snack foods that many children eat (such as potato chips, chocolate, doughnuts, cakes, pastries and cookies). But make an effort to minimize saturated fat and incorporate sources of healthy fats with at least one or two servings from the following every day.

Sources of good fats

* 2 teaspoons of a monounsaturated
  or polyunsaturated margarine
* 2 teaspoons of oil
* 1 tablespoon of salad dressing or mayonnaise
* $1^3/_4$oz of avocado (about one quarter)
* $^3/_4$oz of nuts (about 10 small or 5 large)
* 1 tablespoon of seeds (about the size of a matchbox)
* 1 tablespoon of peanut butter

What do children need to drink?

Water
First preference goes to water. Offer water between meals over any other type of drink. Three-year-olds should be consuming about 3³/₄ cups of fluid per day with about a cup extra (7–10¹/₂fl oz) for every 3 years, up to around half a gallon a day or more for teenagers.

What about bottled water?
Dentists report that tooth decay is making a comeback in children, aided by junk food and snacks and possibly abetted by a surprising culprit—bottled water. Most bottled waters lack the fluoride we get from tap water which helps to prevent tooth decay. So keep bottled water for car trips and sporting events and turn on the tap for a glass of water at home.

Milk
Before 12 months of age, only breastmilk or infant formula is recommended, and for children under 2, full fat milk is best. From 2 to 5 years, reduced fat milk is suitable; skim milk is not appropriate for children under 5. In general, children shouldn't be having more than 2¹/₂ cups of milk a day.

Juice, soft drinks, flavored mineral water and fruit punch
Children don't need any of these to be healthy. They can all reduce a child's appetite, making them picky about eating more nutritious foods at mealtimes. They can also contribute to tooth decay. Keep soft drinks and mineral water as a "sometimes" drink, definitely not every day.

Fruit juice is a source of vitamin C and some plant phytochemicals and is free of artificial colors and flavors. If consumed in excess it can cause diarrhea and contribute to tooth decay and excess calories in children. Keep it to one diluted glass (5–7fl oz) a day or less.

The problem with drinking your calories

Liquid calories are a little stealthier than most, in that they tend to sneak past the satiety center of our brain, which would normally help to stop us from overeating. If consumption figures are any indication, an increase in sugar-sweetened soft drinks and punches is contributing to our child obesity problem. Not only have fatter children been found to have higher consumption of soft drinks, punches and fruit juices, but overall, our children are drinking more of these sweetened drinks than we ever did when we were kids. And of course the increase in serving size from the old fashioned 8fl oz to the current 20fl oz bottle doesn't help.

Treats, fast food and takeout

What sorts of foods are we talking about here? The ones that sit outside the major food groups and are high in saturated fat, sugar or salt, and are low in nutrients. We probably don't need to tell you specifically, but here's a prompt list, just in case: potato chips, candy, punches, commercial cakes and cookies, savory crackers, chocolate, sausage rolls, French fries, burgers, pizza, granola bars, doughnuts, soft drinks, fruit roll-ups, ice cream, jelly. It's not a definitive list because the manufacturers come up with new ones every week!

What to do? Talk to your kids about "treats" or "sometimes foods" versus everyday foods so that they know the difference. Set some guidelines (that you all agree on) about how often to eat these foods. For example, treat foods are those we eat on a special occasion or as a reward for a job well done.

Even better, draw up a list of treats and rewards that have nothing to do with food at all. Here are some ideas to get you started:

* a trip to the beach, park, local swimming pool or amusement park
* a trip to a science museum or the zoo
* having friends to sleep over, or
* new sports equipment.

Healthier takeout options

* Vegetarian Lebanese kebabs—from the falafel to the hummus and the tabbouli, these top the list for healthy, high-fiber, low GI takeout.
* A regular hamburger, including the salad bits!
* Vegetarian nachos—although a little higher in saturated fat, the appeal of the corn chips could make this a winner with kids. It's the beans that are the big bonus and children are usually open to them since they are easy to eat.
* Wraps, rolls and sandwiches incorporating skinless chicken, egg, ham, cheese or salmon with salad.
* Fruit or fruit and nut buns—low GI varieties are available at some bakeries and all make a low fat snack.
* Sushi—another popular and healthy low GI option.
* Noodles or pasta, with seafood, vegetable or meat sauces, are mostly low GI.
* Vegetarian pizza—the fat content varies depending on where you buy it, but it will contribute a few vegetables.
* Milkshakes—a healthy, low GI snack for kids on the go. Ask for skim milk for the over-5s.
* Frozen yogurt.
* Fruit smoothies and ices.

The size of a treat

Ideally, treat foods don't provide more than 10–20 percent of daily calories. This means a daily limit of somewhere between 140–284 cal from treats. That would be the equivalent of one of these:

* a small party-sized sausage roll
* a small serve of French fries
* a small slice of pizza
* 2–3 cups of diluted fruit punch
* a regular can of soft drink
* a 2oz packet of potato chips, corn chips or other starchy snack
* a small cinnamon doughnut
* 2 chocolate cream cookies
* a mini packet of savory crackers
* a soft-serve icecream
* 4 plain sugar cookies
* a medium-sized chocolate bar

Being active

If children get involved in a range of physical activities when they're young, they are likely to continue to be physically active throughout their adult life. Exercise makes children healthier, helps them sleep better and enhances their concentration at school.

Kids might not always hear what you say, but they will definitely watch what you do. So be active yourself and be active with your kids. They will treasure taking a walk or kicking a ball with you, or beating you at a game of table tennis.

It is frightening to know that children absorbed in watching television can burn fewer calories than they do when they are asleep! As a parent you have the right to turn off the television and a responsibility to set limits on your children's TV and computer time. It will benefit everyone in the family to move more and to get active.

Activity pyramid

Use this activity pyramid for children aged 6–12 as a guide to how much activity is recommended. You can create one of your own with your child.

CUT DOWN ON

Screen time

• Watching TV and movies
• Being on the computer more than 30 minutes at a time

2–3 TIMES A WEEK

Do some strengthening exercise and an active hobby

• Gymnastics • Dancing • Hiking
• Push-ups • Martial arts

3–5 TIMES A WEEK

Do something really active for at least 20 minutes

• Aerobics • Running • Cycling • Tennis
• Football • Swimming • Skateboarding

EVERY DAY

Get as much incidental activity as you can

• Make your bed • Get yourself dressed • Walk somewhere
• Put your things away • Play outside
• Help out with household jobs like setting the table, putting away groceries, taking out the trash, feeding pets

Fueling active kids

A young child will believe you if you say "these shoes will help you run faster," so why not use this strategy when it comes to getting them to eat better? If your child enjoys and wants to do well in sports, put the benefits of healthy eating in terms they can relate to. For example, "this fruit will give you energy so you can run faster" or (if you're willing to stretch the truth a little) "eating fish will give you better swimming muscles" and "eating bananas will make you clever as a monkey at gymnastics" and so on.

Of course for an older child, it would probably help if you can convince them that the recipe for the muesli bar you've made is from the Web site of their favorite sporting hero.

Active kids need the same sorts of foods as other children; they just need more of them. In particular, they need more carbohydrate-rich foods because these are their main source of energy. So take food with you to sporting events or training sessions: freshly chopped fruit, sandwiches, muffins, yogurt, milk drinks, fruit juices, sports drinks, fresh bread rolls, etc. And make sure the pantry at home is well stocked with nourishing carbohydrate-rich foods such as bread, breakfast cereals, pasta and rice that can be quickly prepared to satisfy that ravenous appetite upon returning home or to fuel up before running outdoors to play.

Before sports

Low GI carbs are best to give your little athlete extra staying power, for example, yogurt, a sandwich made from low GI bread, low GI breakfast cereals, low GI fruits, milkshakes or 2-minute noodles. This strategy can boost energy levels for longer, strenuous events such as cross-country running or a mini-triathlon. Adequate hydration is important, so aim for around 7fl oz of fluid 1 hour before playing sports.

During sports

Strenuous exercise that lasts more than 90 minutes may necessitate some extra carbs throughout. High GI foods are the obvious choice here to provide an immediate fuel source, but the food needs to be in an easily consumed form so it can be eaten on the run. Generally liquids are best in this situation as they meet fuel and fluid requirements at the same time. Suitable high GI fluids include sports drinks and sweet fruit punches. To maintain hydration, children less than 88lbs should have 3–5fl oz every 20 minutes; children over 88lbs 5–9¼fl oz every 20 minutes. *Always* pack a bottle of drink for training and games.

After sports

The goal here is to replace fluid and energy stores (glycogen) by having some carb-rich foods within 30 minutes of exercising. High GI foods are best at this time because they replenish glycogen faster. Try, for example, rice crackers, jam or honey sandwiches made with white bread, diced watermelon or a bowl of high GI cereal such as Corn Flakes® or Rice Krispies®.

Fluids

Children are at risk of dehydration and heat illness during exercise, and thirst is not an adequate indicator of fluid need when children are playing sports. So make sure they've drunk before they play, take drink breaks during play and top up with extra drinks afterwards.

Coping with food allergies and intolerance

Food allergy, sensitivity and intolerance are terms widely used to refer to an adverse reaction to food. Medically speaking, however, an allergy or hypersensitivity is caused by the immune system whereas intolerance is not. But the symptoms can appear similar, and may include:

* rashes
* swelling of the face and throat
* stomach upset
* dizziness
* headaches, or
* wheezing, congestion and asthma.

Food allergy

Food allergy is increasing and no one quite knows why. If you suspect your child is suffering a food allergy or food intolerance, consult a doctor. The key characteristics of food allergy are:

* symptoms appear very quickly after eating or perhaps even after just touching the food
* symptoms are usually fairly severe and can even be life-threatening, such as anaphylaxis (where the airways close over and breathing is difficult), and
* treatment requires complete avoidance of the problem food.

The foods that most commonly cause allergic reaction in children are peanuts, tree nuts, wheat, eggs, cow's milk and soy. Most children allergic to cow's milk, eggs, wheat or soy will lose their allergies by 3–5 years of age. Allergies to peanuts, tree nuts, fish and shellfish are generally prolonged.

The symptoms of food allergy and food intolerance are shared by many other conditions, so don't rush in and self-diagnose. This is an area where you need to have careful assessment by an experienced medical professional.

What about lactose intolerance?

Lactose intolerance is the inability to digest the sugar, called lactose, found in cow's milk. This means that consuming milk can cause diarrhea, stomach cramping and bloating. Usually small amounts of lactose can be tolerated, for example, cheese (which is virtually lactose-free) and yogurt (the micro-organisms in yogurt are active in digesting lactose during passage through the small intestine). To ensure an adequate calcium intake you could use lactose-free milk or calcium-enriched soy milk.

Preventing food allergy

The chances of children suffering a food allergy are increased if someone else in the family suffers asthma or allergies. There is no real cure for allergy but some steps can reduce the risk.

- Don't smoke during pregnancy, around children or in the spaces where children play or sleep.
- Breastfeed. If it isn't possible to breastfeed and there is a family history of allergy, use a hydrolyzed (hypo-allergenic) formula for the first 6 months of life. Soy and goat's milk formulas are not recommended for prevention of allergy.
- Don't introduce solid foods until 6 months of age.

Should you go gluten-free?

If you or your child have celiac disease, choosing low GI and gluten-free cereal foods can be difficult, as many gluten-free cereals have high GI values. However, virtually all fruits, vegetables, legumes, milk and yogurt are low GI and gluten-free. Here are a few guidelines for selecting lower GI gluten-free options yourself.

Your low GI gluten-free food finder
You'll find that there are many low GI gluten-free foods you can enjoy in four of the five food groups:
* virtually all fruits and vegetables
* whole kernel grains in the breads and cereals group (see opposite)
* legumes of all types in the meat and alternatives group, and
* milk and yogurt among the dairy foods.

What about oats?
To recommend that people with celiac disease avoid oats is controversial because some have been able to eat certain amounts of oats without any damage to their intestinal wall. Oats can add soluble fiber and nutrients to a gluten-free diet. Scientists are currently studying whether people with celiac disease can tolerate oats. Until the studies are complete, people with celiac disease should follow their physician's or dietitian's advice about eating oats.

Which gluten-free breads and cereals to choose?

The key is to look for less processed or refined products if you can—the ones with lots of whole-grain kernels and fiber. Remember, the whole point is to get your stomach to do the processing. Slowly. There are a number of gluten-free breads, breakfast cereals, snack foods and pastas on the market. As not many have been GI tested, here are some guidelines for selecting lower GI options.

Breads: Most of the gluten-free breads tested, including rolls and wraps, have been found to have a high GI. But here is a tip: check out the ingredients list and opt for breads that include chickpea- or legume-based flours and psyllium.

Breakfast cereals: Most gluten-free breakfast cereals, including rice, buckwheat or millet puffs and flakes, have a moderate or high GI because they are refined, not whole-grain, foods. But you can reduce the GI if you serve them with fruit and yogurt and a teaspoon or two of psyllium to boost the fiber.

Noodles: Buckwheat (soba) noodles, cellophane noodles (also known as Lungkow bean thread noodles or green bean vermicelli), made from mung bean flour, and rice noodles, made from ground or pounded rice flour.

What if your child is overweight?

Overweight children need support, acceptance and encouragement from you. They need to know that they are okay whatever their weight. Don't single them out as needing to eat or do things differently from others. Instead, get the whole family living a healthier lifestyle. Here are some ways to make this happen:

* be a good role model in both eating and activity
* talk to your child about health and fitness rather than weight
* eat family meals together at the dinner table
* pack healthy school lunch boxes
* give small servings and allow children to ask for more. This encourages eating to appetite, whereas telling children to eat everything on their plate can lead to overeating
* put no limit on fruit and vegetables
* incorporate filling, low GI foods into the day instead of packaged snacks (see pages 38–39)
* replace juices, fruit punches and sweetened drinks with water or reduced fat milk
* only allow "sometimes" foods *sometimes*, not every day
* don't use food as a punishment or a reward
* focus on reducing sedentary behaviors. Limit TV viewing, computer time and electronic games to a total of two hours per day (combined)
* seek qualified advice from an accredited practicing dietitian. Children younger than high school age don't need to see the dietitian personally as parents are the ones responsible for their eating environment, and
* don't put your child on a diet unless under the guidance of a qualified health professional who has experience in managing childhood obesity. An overweight child may not need to lose a lot of weight but their weight gain may need to slow down while they "grow into" their existing weight.

What if your child is underweight?

Some children are "as thin as a reed" but are active, happy, growing and developing normally. As long as they eat a variety of healthy foods, there is no need to worry. However, you should talk to your doctor if your child has unexpectedly lost weight, stopped gaining weight or has stomach problems like vomiting or diarrhea. When underlying medical concerns have been ruled out, the aim is usually to increase your child's food (read "calories") intake. Here are some healthy ways to do this:

* increase meal frequency—at least three meals and three snacks (or more)
* enforce a stop to play to make time for eating free of distractions
* increase the use of healthy fats (the richest healthy source of calories) with oils, margarines, mayonnaise, salad dressings, avocado and nut spreads
* include a handful or so of nuts in your child's diet daily if possible
* try a fortified milk drink (e.g. Sustagen) or a homemade eggnog with extra skim milk powder if your child is a very picky eater
* foster your child's interest in food by involving them in shopping and cooking
* make sure they're not filling up on drinks. Juice and punch will give a sensation of fullness and take the edge off appetite but contain few calories, and
* don't feed them junk food to promote weight gain. This only teaches them bad eating habits.

What is a healthy weight?

It's impossible to identify a healthy weight for a child that is relevant for any length of time because children are always growing. That's why the weight of children is observed and assessed at a number of intervals over time in conjunction with their height. Growth charts show the range of weight and height expected for a child of a certain age, with separate charts for boys and girls. While you can look at a child and get a pretty good idea of whether they are obviously overweight or underweight, for confirmation a health professional will need to look at the child's body mass index. Body mass index is a measure of weight for height and is calculated by dividing weight (in pounds) by height (in inches squared), multiplied by 705.

Handling picky eaters

Children are capable of learning to like and accept a wide variety of foods and this learning occurs rapidly during the first few years of life. Apparently, by 3 years of age approximately 70 percent of food preferences are established, so early exposure and introduction to a variety of foods is very important.

So exactly how do you get your baby familiar with pumpkin when it seems even the whiff of it makes her mouth clamp shut? You may not want to hear this but you probably need to let her play with it. Food has wonderful tactile properties, and while squeezing it she's also smelling it and that's halfway towards tasting it, so you've progressed up the familiarity scale. As for getting her to taste some off the spoon, you have to try, try and try again. Somewhere between 5 and 10 repeated exposures leads to the doubling of intake of a new food, but research shows that most parents give up after only 2 or 3 attempts.

Another great tactic with some inquisitive infants is to eat whatever you want them to eat yourself, right in front of them. At the very least they'll probably want to handle the food and there you are, notching up another win on the familiarity scale. Be aware that this strategy works in reverse as well, so keep foods you'd prefer they don't have out of sight.

Tips

- Kids tend to need less food than you think, so trust them when they say they're full.
- Eat the same foods that you would like your children to eat.
- Offer lots of opportunities to try new foods. Encourage, but don't force, a small taste.
- To increase consumption of a particular food, repeatedly offer that food on a number of occasions. A young child's acceptance of a food is linked to the amount of exposure they have to it and a food can only become familiar if they see it often.
- Involve kids in food preparation where possible.
- Avoid classifying foods as "good" or "bad" or forbidding certain foods. Instead, teach kids the concept that all foods can be eaten, but with differing frequency. Some foods are for "every day," others are for "sometimes."

What about older children?

As children get a little older, peer pressure seems to kick in, which can be a positive influence and can lead to your child wanting to eat different foods. This works particularly well in group childcare and school settings where perhaps observing their playmates eating new foods convinces them they are safe and worth trying.

At virtually any age, involving kids in food preparation is going to enhance the chances of them wanting to eat whatever's prepared. Part of this is familiarity, part of it is the sense of achievement. Helping you choose the fruit when shopping, then watching you wash and prepare it for their morning snack and being offered taste tests in a relaxed way will enhance acceptance.

Filling hollow legs

The amount of food that is right for your child to eat each day is as individual and changeable as they are. One day you'll be resigning yourself to the fact that young Robbie seems able to obtain nourishment from air, the next day he eats everything you give him with previously unseen efficiency. One thing you can trust in children is their innate ability to respond to the normal signals of hunger and fullness that their body gives them.

When hunger really does hit (as it inevitably will with growth and activity spurts), your child wants to eat and wants to eat now! So make sure you have at the ready some of the low GI favorite stick-to-the-rib foods listed opposite. They'll give your children energy plus nutrients and have what we call the "fill-up factor."

Favorite foods to "stick to the ribs"

Baked beans
Very quick to prepare and always handy to keep in the pantry, baked beans are packed with fiber, protein and vitamins, plus they are easy for a toddler to eat with a spoon or an older child to put on toast.

Oatmeal
Makes a sustaining start to the day for children of all ages. Add fruit yogurt, honey, raisins, frozen berries and banana for variety. For time-poor teenagers, try muesli with a dollop of yogurt.

Pasta and noodles
There's lots of fun to be had in sucking up spaghetti or chasing alphabet pasta around a bowl of soup. Older kids can easily prepare instant noodles and they make a quick, healthy meal with the addition of some frozen mixed vegetables.

Milk
A carton of low fat flavored milk is a nutritious and quick snack for the child on the go, with the goodness of protein, calcium and carbohydrate to satisfy them for longer.

Apples
A crisp little apple is great for school lunch boxes. Have cooked or canned apples on hand for young children and slice them thinly for toddlers. Keep a bowl of washed, fresh apples in the fridge for the most portable, healthy snack for everyone.

Bread
A slice of bread is an excellent (and easy) snack for children of all ages and is so much healthier than cookies and crackers. If you can't get everyone to eat whole-grain, buy a variety of low GI breads on a rotating schedule.

Sweet corn
Suitable as an addition to mashed vegies for a young child, and even a toddler will enjoy munching it off the cob—especially if they've helped prepare it by peeling off the husk.

Ice cream
Low fat ice cream can turn fresh fruit into a delicious, nutritious dessert.

Canned fruits
Ideal for young children and toddlers because it is soft and skin-free. Most children love their own little snack pack of fruit and they are handy for traveling and outings.

menu plans for children

The menu plans in this chapter include the delicious low GI recipes (marked with an asterisk) specially created for children in Part 2 of this book. These menus consist of a variety of simple, healthy meal ideas incorporating lots of fruit and vegetables and emphasizing low GI carbs. You'll even find the odd takeout and the occasional "treat" so you can see exactly how to include these without blowing the nutritional budget.

Consider the quantities of food shown in the menus as a guide. Your child's appetite is the best indicator of the amount of food they need. And remember that it is normal for appetite to vary greatly from one day to the next.

Different menus illustrate how to meet the nutrient needs of children at different ages and stages, including:

* preschool children (2–3 years)
* young school children (4–8 years)
* older school children (9–13 years)
* teenagers (14–18 years).

Include water with meals and snacks where no other drink is mentioned and vary fruit and vegetable choices according to preference and what you have available.

7-day menu Preschool children (2–3 years)

	Monday	Tuesday	Wednesday	Thursday	Friday	Saturday	Sunday
breakfast	1½ high-fiber cereal biscuits with reduced fat milk and a teaspoon of sugar or honey	Banana Porridge* ½ cup of apple juice	Slice of low GI toast topped with hummus, cheese and tomato	Berry Banana Smoothie*	Boiled egg and slice of whole-grain toast spread with margarine ½ cup of orange juice	Apple Porridge*	Slice of French Toast with Honeyed Banana and Passion Fruit Topping* ¾ cup of reduced fat milk
snack	½ pear, sliced ½ banana, sliced	1 kiwifruit 1 cup of reduced fat milk	A slice of fruit bread with margarine	Homemade Popcorn* 1 apple, sliced	½ cup of low fat fruit yogurt with chunks of fruit for dipping	½ slice of Banana Bread*	Chocolate Chip Oat Cookie* 1 cup of reduced fat milk
lunch	Open sandwich of low GI bread topped with hummus and a slice of cheese, 3 or 4 cherry tomatoes and ¼ cup corn kernels	Easy Tomato Tuna Pasta* (half serve) with some sticks of celery and carrot	Chicken and Vegetable Rice-paper Roll*	Whole-grain toast fingers with baked beans	Sandwich of peanut butter and grated carrot	Bite-sized Salmon Cakes* with vegetable sticks (carrot, cucumber, red pepper)	Creamy Chicken and Corn Soup* (half serving)
snack	Slice of fruit bread spread with margarine 1 cup of reduced fat milk	Oat Pikelets* topped with fruit spread	Small 4fl oz carton of reduced fat strawberry-flavored milk	Whole-grain crackers topped with peanut butter Small cup of reduced fat milk	Pineapple and Passion Fruit Juice popsicle*	Nutty Oat Cookie* Small cup of reduced fat milk	Small fruit plate with 3 strawberries, ½ mango and a small cluster of grapes
dinner	Lamb Cutlet with Spiced Pilaf* (half serve) and green beans	Lean beef sausage, slice of whole-grain bread, beetroot slices, carrot sticks and cucumber rounds	Baked Crispy Fish* (half serving) with tomato and cucumber salad and Guacamole* for dipping	Macaroni and Cheese*	Roast chicken with baked potato, pumpkin and peas	Meatballs in Tomato Sauce* with couscous, and steamed broccoli and zucchini	Tuna Barley Bake* (half serving) with green beans
dessert or snack	½ banana with a scoop of low fat ice cream and a drizzle of chocolate sauce	3½oz low fat fruit yogurt	Small bowl of melon chunks	½ cup of canned fruit with ½ cup of low fat custard	Small cup of reduced fat milk	Frozen Berry Yogurt*	Scoop of low fat ice cream in a cone

7-day menu Young children (4–8 years)

	Monday	Tuesday	Wednesday	Thursday	Friday	Saturday	Sunday
breakfast	2 slices of raisin toast spread with margarine 1 cup of low fat milk	High fiber cereal with 1 tablespoon of raisins and reduced fat milk	Crunchy Homemade Cereal* with low fat milk and topped with diced fruit	Low GI toast with ricotta and fruit spread Cup of low fat milk	French Toast* (made with low GI white bread) with cinnamon sugar Glass of low fat milk	Boiled egg with slice of whole-grain toast Small glass of orange juice	Apple Porridge*
snack	Banana	Dried Fruit Pillow* cookie	Mandarin	Celery sticks with reduced fat cream cheese	Oat Pikelets*	Handful of cherries	Fruit Skewers with Passion Fruit Yogurt Dip*
lunch	Thai Chicken Meatballs* in a lettuce leaf with 2 pineapple rings, carrot sticks and 2 or 3 grape tomatoes	Small can of flavored tuna with 6 whole-grain crackers, red pepper and celery strips Small cup of low fat cottage cheese	Pumpkin and Pasta Pie* Small 4fl oz boxed fruit juice	Salmon sandwich on low GI bread Small apple	Low GI sandwich with grated cheese and carrot Apple Small chocolate bar	Tomato and Red Lentil Soup with Toast Fingers*	Children's burger and small French fries
snack	Chocolate Chip Oat Cookie* Slice of watermelon	Slice of low GI toast with their favorite spread Small cup of milk	Nutty Oat Cookie*	Chocolate Hedgehog Slice* 4 or 5 strawberries 1 cup of low fat milk	Homemade Popcorn*	Frozen Berry Yogurt popsicle*	Carrot, celery, cheese and apple sticks
dinner	Macaroni and Cheese*	Lamb Patties with Bulgur*, Sweet Potato Mash* and salad	Beef Stir-fry with Noodles, Corn and Snow Peas*	Vegetarian Tacos*	Pan-fried Fish* on Sweet Potato Mash* with peas or beans	Spaghetti Bolognese*	Easy Fried Rice*
dessert or snack	Small cup of chocolate pudding	Small cup of grapes	3 1/2 oz low fat fruit yogurt	2 scoops of low fat ice cream	Apple and Pear Crumble* with yogurt	Cup of hot chocolate with low fat milk	Sliced peaches with low fat custard

7-day menu School children (9–13 years)

	Monday	Tuesday	Wednesday	Thursday	Friday	Saturday	Sunday
breakfast	Breakfast Couscous* Glass of low fat milk	Whole-grain toast with peanut butter Glass of low fat milk	Whole-grain cereal with raisins and low fat milk	Breakfast Banana Smoothie*	Crunchy Homemade Cereal* with low fat milk	Cinnamon toast made with low GI white bread	Simple Scrambled Eggs* on low GI toast Apple and Mixed Berry Juice*
snack	Low fat fruit yogurt	Hummus* and crackers	Nutty Oat Cookies*	Raisin Banana Bread*	Orange	Trail mix and a banana	Soft-serve frozen yogurt
lunch	Cheese and lettuce sandwich Apple	Individual Ham and Vegetable Frittata* Handful of cherries	Flat bread wrap filled with chicken and salad Small carton of flavored milk	Egg, lettuce and mayonnaise sandwich on low GI bread	Small can of sweet chili tuna, 5 grape tomatoes, carrot and cucumber sticks and a buttered bread roll	Takeout Lebanese kebab	Chicken and Squash Soup with Quinoa* with sourdough garlic bread
snack	Banana on a fresh bread roll	Apricot and Honey Milkshake*	French Toast with Golden Peach Topping*	Wedge of watermelon and a few oat crackers	Honey on low GI toast	Mixed fresh fruit plate	Corn Cakes* with Guacamole*
dinner	Barbecue steak, corn cob, potato salad and coleslaw	Pearl Barley Risotto with Squash and Spinach*	Sang Choy Bau*	Salmon and Pasta Pie*	Homemade pizza	Honey and Oregano Roasted Leg of Lamb* with Roasted Vegetables*	Soy and Sesame Marinated Chicken Drumsticks* with steamed rice, corn and broccoli
dessert or snack	Fruit Skewers with Chocolate Fondue*	Canned pears with low fat custard	Low fat ice cream with pineapple pieces	Raspberry whipped Jell-O made with low fat evaporated milk	Glass of low fat milk	Cup of low fat fruit yogurt	Mango Milkshake*

7-day menu Teens (14-18 years)

	Monday	Tuesday	Wednesday	Thursday	Friday	Saturday	Sunday
breakfast	Whole-grain cereal with low fat milk and banana Carrot, Apple and Celery Juice*	Crunchy Homemade Cereal* with low fat milk and strawberries	Muesli with low fat milk, yogurt and diced peaches	Toast with ricotta, sliced banana and honey	Quinoa Porridge with Pears and Golden Syrup*	Eggs in Nests* Glass of orange juice	Low GI toast with baked beans
snack	Box of raisins, light cheese string and high-fiber crackers	Cinnamon, Polenta and Blueberry Muffin* Snack pack cup of diced peach or pear	Banana	Fruit and Nut Muesli Bar* and a tub of low fat fruit yogurt	Apple	Chocolate Chip Oat Cookies* Skim milk hot chocolate	Mixed dried fruit and nuts Fresh fruit juice
lunch	Chicken, mayonnaise and lettuce sandwich on low GI bread Small carton of low fat flavored milk	Tuna, Tomato, Cucumber and Couscous Salad* Small glass of orange juice	Ham, cheese, and pineapple sandwiches on low GI bread	Smoked Salmon and Cucumber Sushi* Pear	Lebanese bread wrap with Hummus*, tabbouleh and grated cheese 2 fresh plums	Bowl of pasta topped with Easy Tomato Sauce* and grated parmesan Bunch of grapes	Pita bread pizza topped with ham, pineapple, mushroom, onion, pepper and cheese Wedge of melon
snack	Cup of vegetable soup and a slice of toast Apple	Fudgesicle	Full-of-fruit Muffins* Glass of low fat milk	Handful of fresh grapes Bowl of Homemade Popcorn*	Frozen fruit and ice cream bar	Hummus with Tortilla Wedges and Vegetable Sticks*	Oven-baked potato wedges with extra-light sour cream, vegetable sticks and tomato salsa
dinner	Hokkien Noodles with Pork, Vegetables and Egg*	Chicken Curry with Chickpeas, Squash and Spinach*	Takeout Thai beef and noodle salad and 2 or 3 small spring rolls	Bean nachos with Guacamole*	Squash and Spinach Lasagna* with green salad	Barbecued Satay Lamb Kebabs* with rice and snow peas	Steak, Cheesy Vegetable Patties* and Cauliflower and Broccoli Bake*
dessert or snack	Frozen Berry Yogurt*	Mango Milkshake*	Asian fruit salad of lychees, watermelon and nashi pear	Glass of low fat milk	Orange	Bowl of fresh fruit salad and low fat ice cream	Custard Bread Pudding* with light vanilla ice cream

part two

recipes with a
healthy balance

Cooking the low GI way

One of the aims of this book is to show you how to lower the GI of your diet. For those who like to cook, low (or lower) GI recipes are part of the picture. Even if you don't like following recipes, you will find that they give you ideas about how to include low GI foods to make healthy, balanced meals. Besides, the recipes are easy enough for almost anyone to prepare, so call the kids in from playing and get them involved with food! (There's even more chance they'll eat it then, too.)

Naturally we aim to develop recipes with as low a GI as possible, but there are a few popular dishes for which even we find this difficult! Typically these are baked goods made with flour, such as pancakes, muffins and cookies. Because flour is a finely milled product, it is rapidly digested and has a high GI. By incorporating lower GI carbs and lots of fiber into these types of recipes—such as whole kernel grains, rice bran, psyllium husks, fruit, milk and juices—we can lower the GI of these items.

Carbs per serving

We've identified the carbohydrate content of the recipes to assist those with diabetes. For your reference, a slice of bread, a piece of fruit or a cup of milk each contains about 15g of carbohydrate. When a recipe, such as Breakfast Couscous, provides 63g of carbohydrate, this is roughly equivalent to 4 slices of bread (4 x 15g). For recipes serving 4, we've assumed 2 adult servings and 2 child servings (half the size of the adult servings). For recipes serving two or six, we've assumed two or six equal-sized servings, respectively.

Dry/temperature conversions

$1/2$oz	15g
1oz	30g
$1^1/2$oz	45g
2oz	55g
4oz	125g
5oz	150g
$6^1/2$oz	200g
7oz	225g
8oz	250g
1lb	500g
2lb	1kg
300°F	150°C
315°F	160°C
350°F	180°C
375°F	190°C
400°F	200°C
425°F	220°C
450°F	230°C

See page 184 for liquid conversions.

breakfasts and brunches

"Brain-boosting food"

No doubt you know it's a good idea for children to eat breakfast, but did you realize that their food choices can affect their bodies' performances throughout the whole day? To truly nourish and sustain kids' bodies and brains, switch them over to these low GI options.

Breakfast couscous

Serves 2 Preparation time: 5 minutes Cooking time: 1–2 minutes Standing time: 5 minutes
Vegetarian Carbohydrate 63g per serving

This recipe is a good one for kids (or parents) who have to make an early start as you can prepare it the night before. Try topping it with a canned peach half in natural juice, drained and sliced. Although couscous has a medium GI, we have lowered it by adding fruit, orange juice and yogurt in this recipe.

$1/2$ cup freshly squeezed orange juice or unsweetened apple juice

$1/3$ cup water

$1/4$ tsp ground cinnamon

$1/2$ cup couscous

2 tbsp dried apricots or peaches, chopped, or currants

low fat plain yogurt, to serve

3 tsp pure floral honey, or to taste, to serve

2 tbsp slivered almonds, toasted if desired, to serve (optional)

1 Combine the orange juice, water and cinnamon in a small saucepan and bring to a simmer.
2 Combine the couscous and apricots, peaches or currants in a small heatproof bowl and pour over the hot orange juice mixture. Cover the bowl with a plate or plastic wrap and set aside for 5 minutes or until the liquid is absorbed.
3 Meanwhile, combine the yogurt and honey.
4 Use a fork to stir the couscous and separate the grains. Serve topped with the honey yogurt and almonds, if using.

Cook's tip

You can make this the night before and store the couscous and the honeyed yogurt in separate airtight containers in the refrigerator. Warm the couscous gently in a small saucepan over low heat, stirring often with a fork, until heated through.

Banana porridge

Serves 2 Preparation time: 5 minutes Cooking time: 8 minutes
Vegetarian Carbohydrate 31g per serving

Fire up the engine for the day with nourishing, sustaining porridge. For a creamier, richer version, replace the water with reduced fat milk or soy milk and top it with a dollop of low fat vanilla or plain yogurt.

$1/2$ cup rolled oats

$1/4$ cup cold water

1 cup boiling water

1 small banana, sliced, plus extra,
   to serve (optional)

2 tsp pure floral honey, to serve
   (optional)

reduced fat milk or soy milk,
   to serve

1 Combine the rolled oats and cold water in a small saucepan. Add the boiling water and banana and stir well to combine.
2 Bring the porridge to a boil over medium heat, stirring often. Reduce the heat and simmer, stirring often, for 5 minutes or until thick and creamy, adding a little more water if necessary to reach desired consistency.
3 Serve immediately, with extra banana and honey, if using, and milk.

VARIATIONS

Banana and blueberry porridge
Carbohydrate 36g per serving

$1/2$ cup fresh or thawed frozen blueberries

Make the recipe following the method above, adding the blueberries to the porridge just before serving. Serve with honey, if using, and milk.

Apple porridge
Carbohydrate 34g per serving

1 apple, cored, coarsely grated

Make the recipe following the method above, leaving out the banana in Step 1 and stirring apple into the porridge in Step 2, just before serving. Serve with honey, if using, and milk.

Date and maple syrup porridge
Carbohydrate 30g per serving

2 fresh dates, pitted, chopped

2 tsp pure maple syrup, to serve

Make the recipe following the method above, replacing the banana in Step 1 with dates, and the honey in Step 3 with the maple syrup. Serve with extra maple syrup, if desired, and milk.

Quinoa porridge with pears and golden syrup

Serves 4 Preparation time: 5 minutes Cooking time: 15 minutes
Vegetarian and gluten-free Carbohydrate 68g per adult serving

If quinoa is new to you, it's a quick-cooking, grain-like seed that's rich in protein and minerals, low in fat and has a low GI. You'll find it in larger supermarkets (in the health food section) and health food and organic stores. It is very versatile and can be used for breakfast porridge, for main meals as a side dish, to make a risotto, or in salads or desserts.

1 cup quinoa
2 cups reduced fat milk or light soy milk
$^1/_2$ tsp vanilla essence
$^1/_3$ cup currants
warmed reduced fat milk or soy milk, to serve (optional)
2 pear halves in natural juice, sliced, to serve
1 tbsp golden syrup, to serve

1 Place the quinoa in a sieve and rinse well under cold running water. Drain well.
2 Place the quinoa, milk and vanilla essence in a medium-sized saucepan and bring to a boil over medium heat, stirring often. Reduce the heat and simmer, stirring often, for 5 minutes. Add the currants and simmer, stirring occasionally, for 10–12 minutes, or until all of the liquid is absorbed and the quinoa is tender.
3 Spoon the porridge into bowls and serve with a little warmed milk or soy milk, if desired, topped with sliced pear and drizzled with golden syrup.

Cook's tip
Quinoa is cooked when the grain appears translucent and the "germ ring" is visible.

Crunchy homemade cereal

Serves 14—makes 7 cups Preparation time: 10 minutes Cooking time: 30–35 minutes + cooling time
Vegetarian Carbohydrate 29g per 1/2 cup serving

One of the best ways you can lower the overall GI of your family's diet is to substitute high GI foods with low GI alternatives. But not all children like natural or Bircher-style muesli. They want breakfast cereals that crackle and pop! This toasted cereal gives them the best of both worlds—crispy flakes and crunchy rolled oats provide plenty of sound effects and the oat bran boosts the fiber.

3 cups rolled oats
2 cups Special K® cereal
1/2 cup unprocessed oat bran
1/2 cup flaked almonds
1/3 cup unsweetened apple juice
2 tbsp pure floral honey or pure
  maple syrup
1/2 tsp ground cinnamon
1/2 cup raisins or currants (optional)
reduced fat milk or soy milk,
  to serve
low fat plain yogurt, to serve
  (optional)

1 Preheat oven to 325°F and line a large oven tray with parchment paper.
2 Combine the rolled oats, Special K®, oat bran and almonds in a large bowl.
3 Combine the apple juice, honey or maple syrup and cinnamon in a small saucepan and stir over medium heat until well combined. Bring to a simmer then pour over the dry mixture and stir to combine.
4 Spread the mixture evenly over the prepared oven tray and bake for 30–35 minutes or until golden and aromatic, stirring twice during cooking time. Cool on the tray.
5 Add the raisins or currants to the cooled cereal, if using. Serve with reduced fat milk and plain yogurt, if desired.

Cook's tip
Store the cereal in an airtight container at room temperature for up to a month.

French toast with strawberry and banana topping

Serves 2 Preparation time: 5 minutes Cooking time: 4 minutes
Vegetarian Carbohydrate 31g per serving (not including yogurt to serve)

This recipe is a staple at Anneka's house. Her son loves it—mainly for the pancake taste and texture. And Anneka loves it because it is a healthy choice that she can whip up on a busy school morning. It also works well with gluten-free breads.

1 egg
1 tbsp reduced fat milk
$^1/_2$ tsp vanilla essence
1 tsp olive or canola oil margarine
2 thick slices grainy low GI bread, halved
low fat plain yogurt, to serve (optional)

STRAWBERRY AND BANANA TOPPING
$4^1/_2$oz strawberries, hulled and halved
1 banana, sliced
2 tsp pure maple syrup

1 To make the Strawberry and Banana Topping, combine all the ingredients in a small bowl.
2 To make the French Toast, use a fork to whisk together the egg, milk and vanilla in a shallow bowl.
3 Heat a large non-stick frying pan over medium heat. Rub the margarine over the base of the pan. Dip the bread slices in the egg mixture, allowing the bread to soak it up. Remove the bread, allowing any excess egg mixture to drain off. When the margarine is sizzling, add the dipped bread to the pan and cook for 2 minutes each side or until well browned. Serve immediately accompanied by fruit topping and a dollop of yogurt, if desired.

VARIATIONS
Honeyed banana and passion fruit topping
Carbohydrate 32g per serving

1 banana, sliced

pulp of 2 passion fruit

2 tsp pure floral honey

Combine all ingredients in a small bowl and follow the method above.

Golden peach or nectarine topping
Carbohydrate 27g per serving

1 ripe peach or nectarine, pitted, cut into thin wedges

2 tsp golden syrup

Combine all ingredients in a small bowl and follow the method above.

Eggs in nests

Serves 2 Preparation time: 15 minutes Cooking time: 15–20 minutes
Vegetarian and gluten-free (if made with gluten-free bread) Carbohydrate 15g per serving

There are no breakfast skippers when these are on the menu. Children of all ages and stages love "nested eggs" made in a muffin pan. There may not be much time on weekdays for this, but it's a lovely lazy weekend breakfast or brunch when the family is a little more relaxed. Just make double the quantity for 4 people—or for seconds.

2 slices whole-grain bread or similar soft gluten-free bread

olive oil cooking spray

1 tsp olive oil margarine

1^1/$_2$oz button mushrooms (about 4), stems trimmed, sliced

3 English (not baby) spinach leaves, washed, chopped

freshly ground black pepper, to taste

2 eggs

1 tbsp coarsely grated reduced fat cheddar cheese

1 Preheat oven to 350°F.

2 Cut crusts off the bread. Spray both sides of each slice lightly with oil. Press the bread slices firmly into two ^{1}/$_3$ cup capacity non-stick muffin pan holes. Set aside.

3 Heat the margarine in a non-stick frying pan over medium–high heat until sizzling. Add the mushrooms and cook, stirring often, for 4–5 minutes or until tender. Add the spinach and cook, stirring, for 1–2 minutes or until wilted. Remove from heat and season with pepper.

4 Divide mushroom mixture between the bread cases. Crack an egg into a small dish and then slide it into one of the bread cases. Repeat with the remaining egg. Sprinkle with the cheese. Bake for 15 minutes (for a softly set yolk), 20 minutes (for a hard-cooked yolk), or until the egg is cooked to your liking. Serve warm or at room temperature.

Breakfast banana smoothie

Serves 2 Preparation time: 5 minutes
Vegetarian Carbohydrate 27g per serving

Another staple in Anneka's household—quick to make and packed with good things for a solid start to the day. For a non-dairy smoothie, substitute soy milk and soy yogurt. To make a gluten-free smoothie, replace the wheatgerm with almond meal.

1/2 cup reduced fat milk
1/2 cup freshly squeezed orange
  juice
1/4 cup low fat plain yogurt
1 medium ripe banana
2 tsp wheatgerm
2 tsp pure floral honey

Combine all the ingredients in a blender or food processor and blend until smooth. Serve immediately.

VARIATIONS
Berry banana smoothie (pictured right)
Carbohydrate 28g per serving

3 1/2oz fresh or frozen berries

Add the berries to the other ingredients in the blender or food processor and blend until smooth.

Date and banana smoothie
Carbohydrate 28g per serving

4 pitted dried dates or 4 fresh dates, pitted and chopped

If using dried dates, soak them in boiling water for 5 minutes then drain and chop. Omit the honey and add the dried or fresh dates to the other ingredients in the blender or food processor and blend until smooth.

Mango banana smoothie
Carbohydrate 40g per serving

flesh from 1 mango, sliced, or 1 cup diced frozen mango

Add the mango to the other ingredients in the blender or food processor and blend until smooth.

Gluten-free almond cereal

Serves 14—makes 7 cups Preparation time: 10 minutes Cooking time: 20–25 minutes + cooling time
Vegetarian and gluten-free Carbohydrate 20g per ½ cup serving (excluding accompaniments)

If you or your children are on a gluten-free diet, wheat and (possibly) oats are off limits. Here's a crispy, crunchy breakfast cereal that will fuel everyone's day. The apple juice, milk, yogurt and fruit will all help to reduce the GI.

3 cups small puffed rice

3 cups rice flakes

1 cup processed rice bran

⅓ cup sunflower seed kernels

⅓ cup pepitas (pumpkin seeds)

3½oz natural almonds, chopped

⅓ cup unsweetened apple juice

2 tbsp pure floral honey or pure maple syrup

½ tsp ground cinnamon

½ cup currants (optional)

reduced fat milk or soy milk, to serve

low fat plain yogurt, to serve (optional)

fresh or canned peaches, pears or apricots, to serve

1 Preheat oven to 325°F and line a large oven tray with parchment paper.

2 Combine the puffed rice, rice flakes, rice bran, sunflower seed kernels, pepitas and almonds in a large bowl.

3 Combine the apple juice, honey and cinnamon in a small saucepan and stir over medium heat until well combined. Bring to a simmer then pour over the puffed rice mixture and stir to combine.

4 Spread the mixture evenly over the prepared oven tray. Bake for 20–25 minutes, stirring twice, or until lightly golden and aromatic. Cool on tray.

5 Add the currants to the cooled cereal, if using, and serve with reduced fat milk and plain yogurt, if desired, and fresh or canned fruit.

Cook's tip
Store the cereal in an airtight container at room temperature for up to a month.

Shopping tip
You can buy processed rice bran from health food stores and larger supermarkets.

Breakfast fried rice

Serves 4 Preparation time: 5 minutes Cooking time: 10 minutes
Vegetarian Carbohydrate 56g per serving

If you like rice for breakfast, we can recommend this to start your day in a healthy low GI way.

1^1/$_2$ tbsp olive oil
3 eggs, lightly whisked
3 spring (green) onions, trimmed,
  thinly sliced diagonally
3 ripe tomatoes, chopped
4^1/$_2$ cups cooled cooked low GI rice,
  such as basmati
2–3 tbsp salt-reduced soy sauce

1 Heat 2 teaspoons of the oil in a non-stick wok over high heat and swirl around to completely coat the surface. Add half of the egg mixture to coat the inside of the wok. Cook for 2 minutes, or until just set. Carefully remove the omelette from the wok, and repeat with the remaining egg mixture. Roll up both omelettes, cut into thin strips and set aside.

2 Heat the remaining oil in the wok over high heat. Add the spring (green) onions and tomato and cook for 1 minute. Add the rice and toss until heated through. Add the soy sauce to taste, toss gently to combine, and serve immediately topped with the omelette strips.

Cook's tip
If you don't have any leftover rice, cook 1^1/$_3$ cups of uncooked rice. To cool it quickly, spread the rice out over a large tray.

easy egg ideas

Quick mini frittatas

Whisk together 2 eggs with a fork. Stir in 1 small grated zucchini, kernels from
$1/2$ corn cob, $1/3$ cup grated reduced fat cheddar cheese and 2 teaspoons
chopped parsley. Season with freshly ground black pepper.

Spray four $1/3$ cup capacity muffin pan holes with canola or olive oil cooking
spray. Divide the mixture evenly between the muffin pan holes and sprinkle
with a little more grated reduced fat cheddar. Bake in oven preheated to 375°F
for 20 minutes or until just set. Serve warm or at room temperature as a snack
or as a light lunch with salad. **Serves 4**

Simple scrambled egg

Place 2 eggs, 1 tablespoon milk, freshly ground black pepper and 1 teaspoon
chopped parsley in a bowl and whisk with a fork to combine. Melt $1/2$ teaspoon
canola or olive oil margarine in a small non-stick frying pan over medium heat
until foaming. Add the egg mixture and cook for 30 seconds, then use a
wooden spoon to push the egg mixture about 4 times from one side to the
other in different directions, lifting and folding the mixture as you go. Cook for
a further 10 seconds and then repeat the pushing action. Repeat until all the
egg is almost set but still moist. Serve immediately with whole-grain toast.
Serves 2

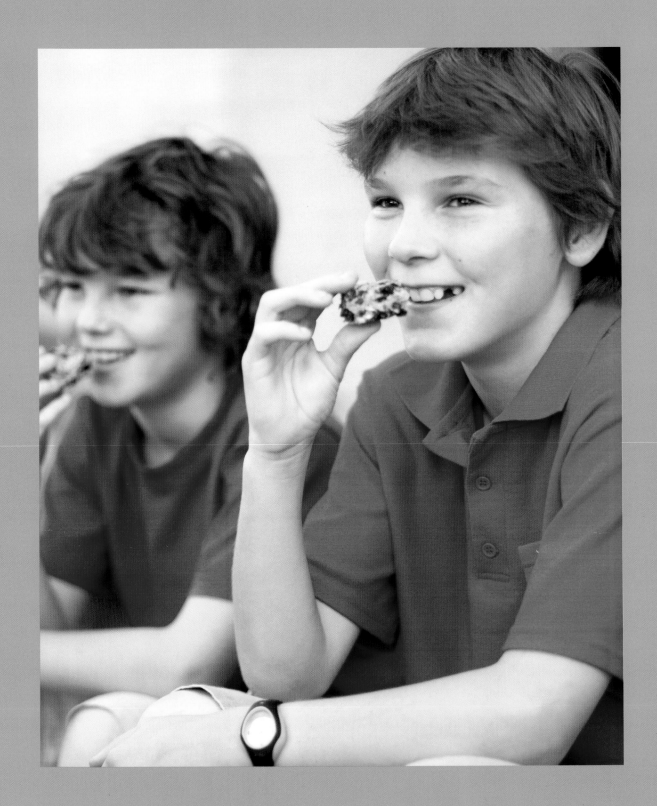

snacks

"If it's healthy, keep it handy"

It's quite normal for children to want to eat every 2 or 3 hours but snacks are much more than just top-ups to the fuel tank. To meet a child's nutrient requirements it's essential that snacks incorporate fruit, dairy and nutritious bread and cereal foods. To step beyond the basics of a slice of bread or piece of fruit, sample some of these ideas.

Hummus with tortilla wedges and vegetable sticks

Serves 4 Preparation time: 10 minutes Cooking time: 15 minutes
Vegetarian and gluten-free (if made with gluten-free corn tortillas) Carbohydrate 18g per adult serving,
9g per child serving

Children seem to enjoy vegetables much more if they are bright, crunchy, and they can use them to dip and scoop to their heart's content. We have suggested vegetable sticks here, but you can cut vegetables into all sorts of shapes. For variety, try other vegetables such as strips of bell peppers, or raw or lightly blanched snow peas, or cauliflower or broccoli florets. This simple recipe is great for an after-school snack or can make a light meal in itself.

1 carrot, peeled, cut into sticks
1 Lebanese cucumber, ends
  trimmed, cut into sticks
1 celery stick, cut into sticks
$^1/_2$ quantity Hummus or Guacamole
  (see recipes page 169)

TORTILLA WEDGES
8in white corn tortillas
olive oil cooking spray

1 To make the Tortilla Wedges, preheat oven to 325°F. Line a large oven tray with parchment paper.
2 Cut each tortilla into 8 wedges, place them on the oven tray and spray them lightly with oil. Bake for 15 minutes or until they are lightly golden and crisp. Cool them on the tray—they will crisp better.
3 Serve Hummus accompanied by the tortilla wedges and vegetable sticks.

Shopping tip
You can also buy hummus from the refrigerator section of supermarkets, fresh produce stores and delis—you will need about $^2/_3$ cup.

Banana bread

Makes 10 slices Preparation time: 20 minutes Cooking time: 50–55 minutes Standing time: 5 minutes
Vegetarian Carbohydrate 26g per serving

Fruit breads like this are a great snack to fill hollow legs and give active kids the energy they need. Enjoy a slice as is, spread with ricotta for an after-school snack, pop a slice in the lunch box for school, or toast a slice and enjoy for breakfast with a dollop of pure fruit spread. Use stale slices to make French toast or a fruity bread and butter pudding.

olive or canola oil cooking spray
3½oz olive oil margarine
¾ cup firmly packed brown sugar
2 eggs
2 large ripe bananas (about 14oz)
⅓ cup buttermilk
1¼ cups plain flour
1½ tsp baking soda
1½ tsp ground cinnamon
½ cup unprocessed oat bran

Cook's tip
To freeze, wrap individual slices in plastic wrap and then seal in a freezer bag or airtight container. Or you can pack the slices in an airtight container and interleave with freezer wrap or parchment paper if you prefer. Thaw slices at room temperature or toast them straight from the freezer.

1 Preheat oven to 350°F. Lightly spray a 8 x 4in loaf pan with oil and line the base and the two long sides with a piece of parchment paper.
2 Combine the margarine and sugar in a large mixing bowl and beat with electric beaters until light and creamy.
3 Add the eggs one at a time, beating well after each addition, until the mixture is pale and fluffy.
4 Mash the bananas and stir into the mixture with the buttermilk using a large metal spoon to combine well.
5 Sift the flour, baking soda and cinnamon together into a mixing bowl, add the oat bran and stir to combine. Add to the banana mixture and fold in until just combined.
6 Spoon into the prepared loaf pan and smooth the surface with the back of a spoon. Bake the banana bread for 50–55 minutes or until a skewer inserted into the center comes out clean. Stand in the pan for 5 minutes before turning onto a wire rack to cool.
7 Store in an airtight container in a cool place (but not in the refrigerator) for up to 4 days.

VARIATIONS

Raisin banana bread
Carbohydrate 33g per serving
½ cup raisins or currants
Make the recipe following the method above adding the raisins with the bananas and buttermilk.

Walnut banana bread
Carbohydrate 26g per serving
1 cup walnut halves, chopped
Make the recipe following the method above adding the chopped walnuts with the bananas and buttermilk.

Oat pikelets

Makes about 24 Preparation time: 15 minutes Standing time: 10 minutes Cooking time: 3–4 minutes per batch
Vegetarian Carbohydrate 8g per pikelet

These are popular for lunch boxes, before or after weekend sports, and as an addition to the birthday party spread. It is easy to whip up a batch (there'll be lots of helping hands) and they have a lovely oaty taste that's delicious with mixed berry spread and a dollop of ricotta. They are also tasty with savory toppings like Guacamole (see recipe page 169) or ricotta and sliced tomato.

3/4 cup plain flour
4 tsp baking powder
1 cup rolled oats
1/4 cup unprocessed oat bran
1 egg
1 1/2 cups buttermilk
canola or olive oil cooking spray
7oz low fat ricotta, to serve (optional)
3 tbsp pure mixed berry spread, to serve

1 Sift together the flour and baking powder into a medium-sized bowl. Stir in the rolled oats and oat bran and then make a well in the center.
2 Use a fork to whisk together the egg and buttermilk then add to the dry ingredients and mix with a large metal spoon until just combined—there will still be a few lumps, but don't worry. Cover and set aside at room temperature for 10 minutes to let the batter thicken slightly.
3 Spray a large non-stick frying pan lightly with oil and preheat over medium heat. Add separate tablespoonfuls of the mixture into the pan to form individual pikelets about 2 1/2in in diameter, spreading the mixture if necessary. Cook for 2 minutes or until bubbles appear on the surface and they are golden brown underneath. Turn the pikelets and cook for a further 1–2 minutes or until just cooked through. Transfer to a wire rack.
4 Repeat with the remaining batter, lightly greasing the pan with the cooking spray between each batch, to make about 24 pikelets in total. Serve warm or at room temperature topped with the ricotta, if using, and the fruit spread.

Cook's tips
- You can make these pikelets up to a day ahead and store them in an airtight container at room temperature.
- To freeze, place in an airtight container with freezer wrap or parchment paper between each layer. Seal and freeze for up to 1 month. Thaw at room temperature.

Full-of-fruit muffins

Makes 24 Preparation time: 20 minutes Cooking time: 20–25 minutes
Vegetarian Carbohydrate 19g per muffin

When you or family members are on the run, top up the tank with these full-of-fruit muffins—ideal for snacks or a breakfast in minutes with a small glass of juice or milk.

2 cups self-raising flour
1 tsp baking powder
1$\frac{1}{2}$ tsp ground cinnamon
$\frac{1}{2}$ cup unprocessed oat bran
1 large ripe banana
1 apple (such as Granny Smith,
   Royal Gala or Golden Delicious),
   unpeeled
5$\frac{1}{4}$oz fresh or thawed frozen mixed
   berries or blueberries
$\frac{1}{2}$ cup pure floral honey
2 eggs, lightly whisked
$\frac{1}{4}$ cup buttermilk
3$\frac{1}{2}$fl oz canola oil

1 Preheat oven to 375°F. Line 2 x 12-hole muffin trays with paper baking cups.
2 Sift together the flour, baking powder and cinnamon into a large mixing bowl. Stir in the oat bran. Make a well in the center and set aside.
3 Use a fork to mash the banana in a medium-sized bowl. Core and coarsely grate the apple and add to the banana. Add the berries, honey, eggs, buttermilk and oil and stir well to combine. Add the fruit to the flour mixture and fold together with a large metal spoon until just combined.
4 Spoon the mixture evenly into the lined pans and bake for 20–25 minutes or until a skewer inserted into one of the muffins comes out clean. Remove from oven and transfer to a wire rack. Serve warm or at room temperature.

Cook's tips
- These muffins will keep in an airtight container at room temperature for up to 2 days.
- To freeze, wrap the muffins individually in plastic wrap and then freeze in sealed freezer bags or an airtight container for up to 1 month. Thaw at room temperature.

Just juice

Serves 1 Preparation time: 5 minutes
Vegetarian and gluten-free

Here's how to make the most of that juice extractor on your countertop and boost your family's fruit and vegetable intake. Apart from fiber, these juicy combos retain many of the nutrients you'd find in the whole fruit. Of course, you can throw in some of the fiber-rich pulp too, if you like. For a longer drink, we suggest serving juices in a large glass topped with sparkling or still mineral water and ice. Make with washed fruits and vegetables just before you serve them. For easy summertime treats you can freeze your children's favorite juice in a popsicle mold.

Carrot, apple and celery juice Carbohydrate 22g per serving

1 carrot
1 apple
1 celery stick

Juice the carrot, apple and celery together.
Pour the juice into a glass and serve with ice, if desired.

Pear and mandarin juice Carbohydrate 27g per serving

1 ripe pear
1 mandarin, peeled

Juice the pear and mandarin together.
Pour the juice into a glass and serve with ice, if desired.

Watermelon, orange and mint juice Carbohydrate 18g per serving

1 cup chopped watermelon flesh, seeds removed
1 orange, peeled
1 sprig of mint

Juice the watermelon, orange and mint together.
Pour the juice into a glass and serve with ice, if desired.

Pineapple and passion fruit juice Carbohydrate 32g per serving

2 cups chopped pineapple flesh (about 2 slices)
1 orange, peeled
pulp of 1 passion fruit

Juice the pineapple and orange together.
Pour the juice into a glass, stir in the passion fruit pulp and serve with ice, if desired.

Apple and mixed berry juice Carbohydrate 39g per serving

2 apples (such as Golden Delicious, Royal Gala or Pink Lady)
4$\frac{1}{2}$oz mixed fresh or thawed frozen berries

Juice the apples and berries together.
Pour the juice into a glass and serve with ice, if desired.

Mango milkshake

Serves 1 Preparation time: 5 minutes
Vegetarian and gluten-free Carbohydrate 46g per serving

By choosing reduced fat varieties of milk and ice cream (or soy alternatives) you create a drink that provides sustained energy and boosts calcium intake but not saturated fat intake. If you opt for soy milk or ice cream, look for calcium-fortified varieties. If there's any left over, freeze as popsicles for after school on hot days.

flesh from 1 mango or 1 cup diced
   frozen mango
$1/2$ cup reduced fat milk or soy milk
2 small scoops reduced fat vanilla
   ice cream or soy ice cream

Place the mango, milk and ice cream in a blender and blend until smooth and frothy. Pour into a tall glass and serve immediately.

VARIATIONS

For many children who don't like the taste of plain milk, adding a little sweetness in the form of fruit or a chocolate powder is a great way to encourage them to increase their dairy intake and build those growing bones. Although some parents may be concerned that flavoring milk with a chocolate powder simply adds extra sugar, it is far more nutritious than a soft drink. Try the options below.

Peachy mango milkshake
Carbohydrate 34g per serving

5oz container diced peach in mango puree

Make following the method above, replacing the mango with diced peach in mango puree.

Apricot and honey milkshake
Carbohydrate 39g per serving

5oz container diced apricot in natural juice (undrained)

1 tsp pure floral honey

Make following the method above, replacing the mango with diced apricot and honey.

Mixed berry milkshake
Carbohydrate 24g per serving

$4^1/2$oz fresh or thawed frozen mixed berries

Make following the method above, replacing the mango with mixed berries.

Homemade popcorn

Serves 2 (makes about 4 cups) Preparation time: 5 minutes Cooking time: 5 minutes
Vegetarian and gluten-free Carbohydrate 18g per serving

Fresh, crunchy homemade popcorn is a quick and easy low GI snack. It's healthy too because you control how much oil and salt you add.

2 tsp vegetable or canola oil
1/4 cup popping corn
1/4 tsp salt (optional)

Place the oil in a heavy-based saucepan with a lid. Heat over medium–high heat until hot and a kernel of popping corn dropped into the saucepan spins in the oil. Add the popping corn, cover and cook over medium–high heat, shaking the pan frequently, until all the corn has popped. Season with salt (if desired) and serve warm or at room temperature.

VARIATIONS

Spiced popcorn

Carbohydrate 18g per serving

1 tsp ground cumin, or to taste

1/4 tsp paprika

Sprinkle the ground cumin and paprika over the warm, cooked popcorn when adding the salt and toss to combine.

Sweet cinnamon popcorn

Carbohydrate 23g per serving

2 tsp icing sugar

1 tsp ground cinnamon

Omit the salt. Sift the icing sugar and cinnamon over the warm, cooked popcorn and toss to combine.

Cook's tips

- Use a heavy-based saucepan; for example, cast iron or one with a "sandwiched" base. These pans distribute heat evenly and will help you successfully prepare popcorn without a fuss. Wear oven mitts to shake the pan back and forth.
- You can make popcorn up to 3 days ahead of serving. To keep fresh, store in an airtight container at room temperature.

Nutty oat cookies

Makes about 40 Preparation time: 15 minutes Cooking time: 20 minutes + cooling time
Vegetarian Carbohydrate 15g per serving (2 cookies)

These cookies are rich in fiber and packed with nuts and seeds. Sifting the flour will get rid of any lumps, but it's important you return any husks to the bowl for that essential fiber. This is a fun, hands-on family recipe as there's lots to do for children who love to help with baking, from sifting the flour to rolling the mix into balls and flattening them into cookies. They are very tempting, but remember, a serve is 2 cookies!

1 cup plain whole-grain flour
1 tsp ground cinnamon
1¼ cups rolled oats
⅓ cup firmly packed brown sugar
¼ cup chopped walnuts
2½ tbsp pepitas (pumpkin seeds)
2 tbsp sunflower seed kernels
4 tsp sesame seeds
3½oz olive oil or canola margarine
¼ cup golden syrup
2 tbsp water
1 tsp baking soda

1 Preheat oven to 325°F. Line 2 large baking trays with parchment paper.
2 Sift the flour and cinnamon together into a large mixing bowl, returning any husks to the flour. Stir in the rolled oats, brown sugar, walnuts, pepitas, sunflower seed kernels and sesame seeds and set aside.
3 Combine the margarine, golden syrup and water in a small saucepan. Warm gently over a medium heat, stirring occasionally, until the margarine melts. Remove from the heat and stir in the bicarbonate of soda. Add immediately to the dry ingredients and stir with a wooden spoon to combine.
4 With damp hands, roll walnut-sized portions of the mixture into balls and place about 2in apart on the lined oven trays. Flatten each ball to about 1½in in diameter. Bake for 20 minutes or until cooked through and beginning to darken around the edges, swapping the trays halfway through the cooking time.
5 Remove from oven and stand on the trays for 5 minutes before transferring to a wire rack to cool completely.

Cook's tip
Store cookies in an airtight container at room temperature for up to a week.

Fruit and nut muesli bars

Makes 20 bars Preparation time: 20 minutes Cooking time: 35 minutes
Vegetarian Carbohydrate 12g per serving

You can't beat homemade muesli bars. There's a whole heap of benefits from these ones, packed as they are with fruits, nuts, seeds, rolled oats, good fats and no added salt.

1 cup rolled oats

1 cup Rice Krispies®

$^1/_2$ cup unprocessed oat bran

$^1/_2$ cup currants

$^1/_3$ cup dried apricots or peaches, finely chopped

$^1/_3$ cup natural almonds, finely chopped

$^1/_4$ cup brazil nuts, finely chopped

$^1/_4$ cup sunflower seed kernels

2 tbsp linseeds (flaxseeds)

$^1/_4$ cup pure maple syrup

2 tbsp olive or canola oil margarine

2 eggs, lightly whisked

1 Preheat oven to 350°F. Line the base and long sides of a 6 x 10in (base measurement) non-stick slice pan or a 8in square shallow cake pan with parchment paper.

2 Combine the rolled oats, Rice Krispies®, oat bran, currants, apricots, almonds, brazil nuts, sunflower seed kernels and linseeds (flaxseeds) in a large bowl.

3 Mix the maple syrup and margarine in a small saucepan over medium heat until simmering. Reduce the heat and simmer for 1 minute. Add to the dry ingredients with the eggs and stir to combine evenly.

4 Spoon the mixture into the prepared pan and press with the back of a spoon to smooth the surface. Bake for 35 minutes or until set and golden on top. Cool completely in the pan. Cut into 20 bars.

Cook's tip
Store in an airtight container at room temperature for up to 2 weeks.

easy canned fruit ideas

Apricot smoothie

Blend 1 x 5oz container diced apricot (with its natural juice), $1/2$ ripe banana, 1 large spoonful reduced fat vanilla yogurt, $1/2$ teaspoon vanilla essence and a pinch ground cinnamon until smooth and frothy. Serve immediately. **Serves 1**

Fruity dessert parfaits

Layer slices of canned peach, plum, pear or apricot with reduced fat vanilla or strawberry yogurt and finish with a layer of sliced strawberries. Then drizzle a little honey over the strawberries and sprinkle with toasted raw nuts and seeds.

Peach slushie

Drain 1 x 15oz can peaches (in natural juice) and blend with 2 scoops of frozen vanilla, mango or berry yogurt and 1 cup of ice until smooth and icy. Serve immediately. **Serves 2**

Fruity English muffin

Toast a whole-grain English muffin and spread with low fat ricotta, top with sliced canned peach or apricot, drizzle with a little pure floral honey and dust lightly with ground cinnamon.

lunch

"It's a vital part of the day"

What parent doesn't struggle sometimes deciding what to give their child for lunch? A good basic formula is low GI carb + protein + fruit and vegetables, but there's a world of variations on this as you'll see in the following pages.

Vegetable rice-paper rolls

Serves 6 (makes 12) Preparation time: 30 minutes
Vegetarian and gluten-free (if using gluten-free soy and sweet chili sauces) Carbohydrate 15g per serving

Everyone loves to wrap and roll, making this family favorite a real hands-on effort that's ideal for light meals, lunches and snacks.

3oz rice vermicelli

4 tsp salt-reduced soy sauce

1 tsp freshly sqeezed lemon juice

12 x 8½in round rice-paper wrappers

1 small Lebanese cucumber, halved and each half cut into 12 thin wedges

1 carrot, peeled, cut into thin matchsticks

1 red pepper, deseeded, cut into thin strips

1 cup bean sprouts

1 small bunch mint or cilantro, leaves picked (optional)

salt-reduced soy sauce and/or sweet chili sauce, to serve

1 Place the vermicelli in a medium-sized heatproof bowl and pour over enough boiling water to cover. Set aside for 5 minutes or until the noodles are tender. Drain well and return noodles to the bowl. Combine the soy sauce and lemon juice, add to the noodles and toss to combine. Set aside to cool.

2 Fill a large bowl with very warm water and dip a rice-paper wrapper into the water until pliable but not too soft (10–30 seconds, depending on the brand of the wrappers and the heat of the water). Remove the wrapper from the water and place on a double-thickness of paper towel.

3 Place a little of the vermicelli across the center of the wrapper, leaving about ³/₄in at each end. Top with 2 wedges of cucumber, a little carrot, pepper and bean sprouts, and a few mint or cilantro leaves (if using). Fold in the ends of the wrapper and then roll up tightly to enclose the filling. Place on a plate and cover with damp paper towel. Repeat with remaining wrappers and filling ingredients. Serve cut in half with soy sauce and/or sweet chili sauce (or a combination of both).

VARIATIONS

Rice-paper rolls don't have to be vegetarian. Try adding chicken or beef. Here's what you need to make 12 rolls.

Chicken and vegetable

Carbohydrate 15g per serving

1 skinless chicken breast, poached or roasted (or leftover barbecued chicken with no stuffing)

Use 2 forks or your fingers to shred the chicken and add a little to each roll before wrapping up.

Beef and vegetable

Carbohydrate 15g per serving

2 small (about 6oz each) New York cut (boneless sirloin) steaks

Chargrill the steaks over a medium–high heat until cooked to your liking. Rest for 10 minutes. Cut into thin slices across the grain and add a few pieces to each roll before wrapping up.

Cook's tips

- The rolls can be made the day before and stored in the refrigerator in an airtight container lined with damp paper towel. Cover the rolls with more damp paper towel and seal.
- For school lunches, transport in an insulated bag with an icepack.

Ham and vegetable frittata

Serves 4 Preparation time: 10 minutes Cooking time: 20–25 minutes
Gluten-free Carbohydrate 15g per adult serving, 8g per child serving

Frittatas are great for using up whatever vegetables you have in the refrigerator or freezer. The trick is to keep it colorful. Try peas, corn, chopped cooked spinach or red pepper, for a change. For a vegetarian version, simply leave out the ham.

9oz orange sweet potato or deseeded squash, peeled, cut into $1/2$in pieces

4 eggs

2 tbsp reduced fat milk

2 tbsp flat-leaf (Italian) parsley, chopped (optional)

$1/2$ cup coarsely grated reduced fat cheddar cheese

freshly ground black pepper, to taste

olive oil cooking spray

$3^1/2$oz sliced lean ham, chopped

1 medium zucchini, sliced into $1/4$in rounds

3 spring (green) onions, finely sliced

$4^1/2$oz cherry or grape tomatoes, halved

1 Boil or steam the sweet potato or squash for about 4 minutes or until just tender. Drain well.

2 Place the eggs, milk, parsley (if using) and half the cheese in a medium-sized bowl and whisk with a fork until combined. Season with pepper and set aside.

3 Lightly spray a 8in (base measurement) non-stick frying pan with oil and heat on medium. Add the ham and zucchini and cook for 5 minutes, stirring often, or until the ham starts to color and the zucchini to soften. Add the sweet potato and spring onions and cook, stirring occasionally, for 2 minutes.

4 Spread the mixture evenly over the base of the pan and arrange the tomatoes over the top, cut side up, pressing them gently into the vegetables. Carefully pour the egg mixture over the vegetables and cook on medium heat for 5–8 minutes, or until almost set.

5 Meanwhile, preheat the grill on high. Sprinkle the remaining cheese over the frittata and cook under the grill for 3–5 minutes until the egg mixture is just set and the frittata is lightly golden on top. Serve warm, or cool in the pan and serve at room temperature.

VARIATION

Individual ham and vegetable frittatas

Carbohydrate 5g per frittata

Makes 8 Preparation time: 15 minutes Cooking time: 30–35 minutes

1 Preheat oven to 350°F. Lightly spray 8 holes of a $1/3$ cup non-stick muffin pan with oil.

2 Instead of spreading the vegetable mixture over the base of the frying pan (Step 4), stir the cooked vegetables and ham into the whisked egg mixture and then spoon into the muffin holes. Top each with tomato halves and a little cheese.

3 Bake for 20–25 minutes or until lightly golden on top and cooked when tested with a skewer.

Cook's tips

- If you make the frittata a day ahead, store in an airtight container in the refrigerator.
- For school lunches, pack in an airtight container in an insulated bag with an icepack.

Easy tomato tuna pasta

Serves 4 Preparation time: 10 minutes Cooking time: 15 minutes
Carbohydrate 52g per adult serving, 26g per child serving

What's for lunch? This is the perfect "from the pantry" meal made in minutes with a can of tomato soup, a can of tuna and pasta. We have used macaroni, but you can use your favorite short pasta shape. You can even whip it up a day ahead.

6$\frac{1}{2}$oz good-quality dried macaroni
   pasta

1 small brown onion, finely chopped

$\frac{1}{4}$ cup water

10$\frac{1}{2}$oz can tomato soup
   (see Shopping Tip below)

15oz can tuna in oil, drained, flaked
   into chunks

freshly ground black pepper, to
   taste

1 cup coarsely grated reduced fat
   cheddar cheese

mixed green salad (or carrot,
   cucumber and celery sticks, for
   younger children), to serve

1 Cook the pasta in a large saucepan of boiling water following the packet directions, or until al dente. Drain.
2 Meanwhile, combine the onion and water in a medium saucepan, cover and cook over medium heat, stirring occasionally, for 8–10 minutes or until the onion is soft.
3 Add the tomato soup to the onion and bring to a simmer over medium heat. Add the pasta and heat through. Stir in the tuna and half the cheese. Serve topped with the remaining cheese and the salad or vegetables.

Cook's tips
- Store any leftovers in an airtight container in the refrigerator for up to 1 day.
- Reheat in a saucepan over medium heat, stirring often, until heated through.

Shopping tip
This recipe is best made with a "creamy tomato" or "cream of tomato" soup.

Tuna, tomato, cucumber and couscous salad

Serves 4 Preparation time: 10 minutes Standing time: 15 minutes
Carbohydrate 52g per adult serving, 26g per child serving

For a change of flavor, replace the tuna with a can of red or pink salmon, drained, skin discarded and flaked.

1 cup good-quality couscous
1/2 cup cold water
1/3 cup fresh orange juice, strained
15oz can tuna in oil, drained, flaked into chunks
9oz punnet cherry or grape tomatoes, halved (quartered if large)
1 Lebanese cucumber, quartered lengthwise and cut into 1/2in slices
2 spring (green) onions, thinly sliced
2 tbsp chopped mint (optional)
freshly ground black pepper, to taste
4 tsp lemon juice, or to taste

1 Combine the couscous, water and orange juice in a small bowl and set aside for 15 minutes or until all the liquid has been absorbed.
2 Use a fork to stir the couscous and separate the grains. Add the tuna, tomatoes, cucumber, spring onions, mint (if using) and pepper to taste. Toss gently to combine, taste and adjust seasoning with lemon juice, if desired.

Cook's tips
- If you make the salad a day ahead, store overnight in an airtight container in the refrigerator.
- For lunch boxes, pack in an airtight container in an insulated bag with an icepack. Don't forget to include a fork!

Salmon and pasta pie

Serves 6 Preparation time: 20 minutes Cooking time: 1 hour Standing time: 5 minutes
Carbohydrate 23g per serving

It's easy to ring the changes with this family stand-by and create a meal with a completely different flavor. And kids who aren't that keen on veggies won't even know there is zucchini in it.

canola or olive oil cooking spray

5$\frac{1}{4}$oz good-quality short pasta
(such as penne or shells)

4$\frac{1}{4}$oz shortcut bacon slices
(about 4), all fat removed, chopped

7$\frac{1}{2}$oz can no-added-salt red or pink
salmon, drained, skin removed
and flesh coarsely flaked

3 medium zucchinis, coarsely grated

$\frac{3}{4}$ cup coarsely grated reduced fat
cheddar cheese

4 spring (green) onions, thinly sliced

freshly ground black pepper,
to taste

4 eggs

2 egg whites

$\frac{1}{4}$ cup self-raising flour, sifted

mixed salad, to serve

1 Preheat oven to 350°F. Spray an 8in springform pan with canola or olive oil and line the base with a piece of parchment paper.
2 Cook the pasta in a large saucepan of boiling water following the packet directions, or until al dente. Drain well and set aside.
3 Meanwhile, cook the bacon in a small non-stick frying pan over medium–high heat, stirring occasionally, for 2–3 minutes or until starting to brown. Combine the bacon, pasta, salmon, zucchini, two-thirds of the cheese and the spring onions in a large bowl. Season well with pepper.
4 Use a fork to lightly whisk the eggs and egg whites to combine. Whisk in the flour. Add to the pasta mixture and use a large metal spoon or a spatula to stir until just combined.
5 Spoon the mixture into the prepared pan and smooth the surface. Sprinkle with the remaining cheese and bake for 50 minutes or until lightly golden and just set in the center. Remove from oven and stand in pan for 5 minutes before transferring to a wire rack. Serve warm or at room temperature cut into wedges.

VARIATIONS

Squash and pasta pie Carbohydrate 28g per serving

$\frac{1}{2}$ small butternut squash (about 1lb 2oz)

Omit the salmon. Peel, deseed and cut the squash into $\frac{3}{4}$in pieces. Boil or steam the squash for 4 minutes or until just tender. Drain well and add to the mixture before the eggs and proceed with the recipe.

Individual salmon and pasta pies Carbohydrate 17g per serving

Makes 8 Preparation time: 20 minutes Cooking time: 35–40 minutes
Standing time: 5 minutes

Preheat oven to 375°F. Lightly spray 8 holes of a 1 cup capacity non-stick muffin pan with olive or canola oil. Follow the basic method and then spoon the mixture into the muffin pan and bake for 35–40 minutes or until lightly golden on top.

Cook's tips
- If you make the pie a day ahead, store in an airtight container in the refrigerator.
- For lunch boxes, pack in an airtight container in an insulated bag with an icepack.

Tuna and cucumber sushi

Makes 32 pieces Cooking time: 15 minutes Standing time: 10 minutes Cooling time: 30 minutes Preparation time: 25 minutes
Carbohydrate 7g per serving

Sushi may seem fiddly, but once you have mastered the basics you will never look back. It's a great hands-on recipe for the whole family. Leave any leftover sheets of nori in the packet with the moisture-absorbing sachet and store in a resealable plastic bag to prevent them from softening.

1 large Lebanese cucumber

4 sheets sushi nori

6oz can tuna in springwater,
   drained, flaked into small chunks

1/2 red bell pepper, deseeded, cut
   into thin strips

soy sauce, to serve

pickled ginger, drained, to serve

SUSHI RICE

1 1/4 cups Koshihikari (sushi) rice

1 3/4 cups water

2 1/2 tbsp sushi vinegar

HAND VINEGAR

1 cup water

2 tbsp sushi vinegar

1 To make the Sushi Rice, place the rice and water in a medium saucepan with a tight-fitting lid and bring to a boil. Reduce to the lowest possible heat and cook for 12–15 minutes, or until all the water has been absorbed. Set aside, still covered, for 10 minutes. The rice should be slightly sticky but not mushy.

2 Transfer the rice to a large shallow dish and sprinkle with the sushi vinegar. Use a spatula or large spoon to fold the vinegar through the rice (do not stir as the rice grains will break up and become pasty). Set the rice aside, uncovered, for 30 minutes or until cooled to room temperature.

3 Halve the cucumber lengthwise and scoop out the seeds with a teaspoon. Cut each half lengthwise into 4 thin wedges.

4 To make the Hand Vinegar, combine the water and vinegar in a medium-sized bowl. (Use this mixture to dip your hands in while making the sushi as the rice will stick to anything that isn't moist.)

5 Place a bamboo sushi mat with the slats running horizontally on a work surface. Place a sheet of nori, smooth side facing downwards and faint lines horizontal, on the mat about 3/4in from the front edge of the mat. Dip into the hand vinegar mixture then

scoop out a quarter of the cooled rice and spread it evenly over the nori sheet, leaving a ¾in-wide strip of uncovered nori at the far end. Place 2 wedges of cucumber and a quarter of the pepper strips across the nori sheet about a third of the way up from the bottom edge. Top with a quarter of the tuna.

6 Use your thumbs and forefingers to pick up the bottom end of the bamboo mat and use your other fingers to hold the fillings in place while lifting the mat over to enclose. Continue to roll the nori and fillings, gently pulling the mat to make a firm roll, to join the uncovered strip of nori at the far side. Use the mat to gently pull and tighten the roll again. Unroll the mat and wrap the finished sushi roll in plastic wrap. Repeat to make 3 more rolls.

7 To slice, wipe a sharp knife on a cloth dipped into hand vinegar and cut the rolls into 8 equal portions, wiping the knife with the cloth between each cut. Serve accompanied by the soy sauce for dipping and pickled ginger, if desired.

OTHER FILLINGS

- Cucumber and avocado
- Canned salmon, carrot and bell pepper
- Smoked salmon and cucumber
- Shrimp, cucumber and avocado

Cook's tips

- You can make the sushi rice up to 5 hours ahead and store covered with damp paper towel and then plastic wrap in the refrigerator.
- Cover sushi rolls in plastic wrap and keep in the refrigerator for up to 1 day.

Tomato and red lentil soup with toast fingers

Serves 4 Preparation time: 15 minutes Cooking time: 30–35 minutes
Vegetarian and gluten-free (if made with gluten-free bread) Carbohydrate 33g per serving (including bread)

This simple and tasty soup is a great way to get in those extra serves of vegetables along with some lentils—nutritional power packs that give kids (and parents) lasting energy. Try it with a dollop of reduced fat plain yogurt.

1 brown onion, chopped
1 medium carrot, peeled, chopped
1 celery stick, chopped
2 garlic cloves, crushed
1/4 cup water
2 tsp ground cumin
1/2 tsp paprika (optional)
14oz can no-added-salt
  diced tomatoes
1 tbsp no-added-salt tomato paste
1/2 cup split red lentils
3 cups salt-reduced vegetable stock
2 tsp sugar, or to taste
freshly ground black pepper,
  to taste

TOAST FINGERS
4 slices multigrain or gluten-free low
  GI bread
2 tsp olive or canola oil margarine

1 Combine the onion, carrot, celery, garlic and water in a large saucepan. Cover and cook over medium heat, stirring occasionally, for 8–10 minutes or until the onion is soft. Stir in the cumin and paprika (if using) and cook, uncovered, for 1–2 minutes or until the water has evaporated.

2 Add the canned tomatoes, tomato paste, lentils and stock and bring to a simmer. Reduce heat to low, cover partially, and simmer gently, stirring occasionally, for 20 minutes or until the lentils are tender.

3 Meanwhile, to make the toast fingers, preheat oven to 400°F and line an oven tray with non-stick parchment paper. Spread both sides of the bread slices with the margarine and cut each into 3 fingers. Place the bread on the lined oven tray. Just as the lentils are becoming tender, bake the bread for 10 minutes or until lightly golden and crisp. Turn off oven and leave it there to keep warm.

4 Transfer half the soup mixture to a blender or food processor and blend until smooth. Repeat with remaining mixture. Return the soup to the pan and simmer gently until heated through or until reduced to desired consistency. Taste and season with sugar and pepper. Serve accompanied by the warm toast fingers for dipping.

Cook's tips
- If you make the soup a day or two ahead, keep in an airtight container in the refrigerator. Reheat in a saucepan over medium heat, stirring frequently, until simmering and heated through.
- Freeze leftovers in serving portions in airtight containers for up to 2 months. Thaw in the refrigerator before reheating.

Creamy chicken and corn soup

Serves 4 Preparation time: 10 minutes Cooking time: 15–20 minutes
Carbohydrate 22g per serving

Soup is a natural winter warmer that's enjoyed year round whenever comfort food is the order of the day. Whisk a beaten egg into the soup just before serving—it may look a little curdled but will still be delicious and it makes it even more nutritious.

9oz trimmed chicken tenderloins or breast fillet

2 cups salt-reduced chicken stock

3 cups water

3½oz short vermicelli pasta (see Shopping Tip below)

4½oz can creamed corn

freshly ground black pepper, to taste (optional)

3 spring (green) onions, finely sliced on the diagonal, to serve

1 Place the chicken in a medium saucepan. Add the stock and water and bring to a simmer over medium heat. Reduce to low and poach gently until the chicken is just tender (about 1 minute for tenderloins or 4–5 minutes for a whole chicken breast). Use a slotted spoon to transfer the chicken to a plate and set aside to cool slightly.

2 Bring the stock back to a boil. Add the vermicelli and boil for 6–8 minutes, or until al dente.

3 Meanwhile, use 2 forks or your fingers to shred the chicken. Add the creamed corn and shredded chicken to the soup and cook until just heated through. Taste and season with pepper (if using). Serve immediately garnished with spring onions.

VARIATION
Clear chicken noodle soup
Carbohydrate 24g per serving

1 large corn cob

4 cups salt-reduced chicken stock

1 cup water

Follow the cooking instructions above, replacing the creamed corn with the kernels from the large corn cob, and use 4 cups of chicken stock and 1 cup of water for the liquid.

Shopping tip
If you can't find short vermicelli pasta (it may be called filini vermecelles) use vermicelli pasta broken into 2in lengths.

Cook's tip
If you make the soup a day ahead, store overnight in an airtight container in the refrigerator. Reheat in a saucepan over medium heat, until just heated through. The vermicelli will absorb some of the liquid on standing so you may add a little more stock and/or water to reach desired consistency.

Lunch box basics

School lunches don't have to be difficult. Add some fruit and a bottle of water to any lunch box and you've mastered the art of feeding your child at school. Use this formula as a quick guide:
Base + Filling + Vegetables

Whole-grain roll + tuna + lettuce and avocado

Low GI bread + cheese + a box of salad vegetables

Yukon Gold potato salad + hard-boiled egg + lettuce, celery and cucumber

Three-bean mix + feta cheese cubes + Greek salad

Flat bread + diced chicken + salad

easy ways with legumes

Baked bean toasted sandwich

Sandwich canned baked beans and a little reduced fat cheddar cheese between 2 slices of whole-grain bread. Cook in a non-stick sandwich maker until toasted and heated through. Serve warm.

Beef and lentil burgers

Add canned brown lentils, drained and rinsed, to your favorite hamburger patty mixture. Allow a 14oz can for every $17^{1}/_{2}$oz lean ground beef to serve 6 people.

Vegetable soup with beans

Add a can of kidney or cannellini beans or chickpeas, drained and rinsed, to your favorite vegetable soup (such as minestrone) at the end of cooking.

Roasted vegetables with chickpeas

Toss drained and rinsed canned chickpeas through roasted vegetables towards the end of cooking. Sprinkle with chopped fresh herbs such as basil or flat-leaf (Italian) parsley and serve with roasted or grilled meats.

main dishes

"Much depends on dinner"

Setting the table, turning off the TV and eating a meal together is one of the most important, regular things you can do with your children. Family meals offer the opportunity to make healthy eating normal. Research has shown that children who have regular family dinners eat more fruit and vegetables, more fiber, fewer fried foods and are less likely to be overweight than those who don't. So gather them around the table for these super-nutritious dinners.

Chicken curry with chickpeas, squash and spinach

Serves 4 Preparation time: 15 minutes Cooking time: 20–25 minutes
Gluten-free (if using a gluten-free curry paste) Carbohydrate 82g per adult serving, 41g per child serving

We made this with light coconut milk. For even less fat, try using coconut-flavored evaporated milk, available from supermarkets.

1 brown onion, finely diced

¼ cup water

¼ cup red curry paste, or to taste

18oz chicken thigh fillets, fat trimmed and flesh cut into 1in pieces

½ butternut squash, peeled, deseeded, cut into 1in pieces

14oz can no-added-salt diced tomatoes

1 cup salt-reduced chicken stock

⅓ cup light coconut milk

14oz can chickpeas, drained, rinsed

3½oz baby spinach leaves

1 cup basmati, or other low GI rice, cooked following packet directions, to serve

steamed green beans or peas, to serve

1 Combine the onion and water in a medium-sized saucepan and cook, covered, over medium heat, stirring occasionally, for 8–10 minutes or until the onion is soft. Add the curry paste and cook, stirring, for 2–3 minutes or until aromatic.

2 Add the chicken and squash and stir to coat with the curry paste. Add the tomatoes, stock and coconut milk and bring to a simmer over medium heat. Reduce heat and simmer gently for 20 minutes or until the squash is just tender.

3 Stir in the chickpeas and spinach and simmer for 2 minutes, stirring occasionally, or until the spinach has just wilted. Serve immediately accompanied by the cooked rice and vegetables.

VARIATION
Chickpea, squash and spinach curry

Vegetarian and gluten-free (if using a gluten-free curry paste)
Carbohydrate 105g per adult serving 53g per child serving

1 butternut squash, peeled, deseeded, cut into 1in pieces

2 x 14oz cans chickpeas, drained, rinsed

Replace the chicken with extra squash and chickpeas and follow the method above.

Cook's tip
Store in an airtight container in the refrigerator for up to 2 days. Reheat in a saucepan over medium heat, stirring frequently, until just heated through.

Tuna rice bake

Serves 6 Preparation time: 20 minutes Cooking time: 35 minutes
Carbohydrate 26g per serving

Any leftovers of this oven-to-table favorite will keep overnight covered with plastic wrap or in an airtight container in the refrigerator. Simply uncover and reheat in the dish in an oven preheated to 325°F for 25–35 minutes or until heated through.

1 brown onion, finely chopped

¼ cup water

1 quantity Cheese Sauce (see recipe page 172)

2 tbsp reduced fat milk

2 cups cooked low GI rice, such as basmati

2 x 6½oz cans tuna in olive oil, drained, coarsely flaked

2 tbsp chopped flat-leaf (Italian) parsley

freshly ground black pepper, to taste

1 cup firmly packed breadcrumbs (from day-old multigrain or sourdough bread)

olive oil cooking spray

steamed, boiled or microwaved green beans and quartered yellow squash, to serve

1 Preheat oven to 400°F.

2 Combine the onion and water in a medium saucepan and cook, covered, over medium heat, stirring occasionally, for 8–10 minutes or until the onion is soft. Add the Cheese Sauce and milk and cook over medium heat, stirring often, until heated through.

3 Transfer the sauce to a medium-sized bowl and add the cooked rice, tuna and parsley. Taste and season with pepper. Spoon the mixture into a 6 cup ovenproof dish. Sprinkle breadcrumbs over the top and then spray them lightly with the olive oil for a crunchy topping.

4 Bake for 20 minutes or until heated through and the top is golden and crisp. Serve warm with the beans and squash.

VARIATION
Tuna barley bake
Carbohydrate 24g per serving

⅔ cup pearl barley

Cook the pearl barley in boiling water for 45–50 minutes or until tender. Make the recipe in the same way, replacing the rice with pearl barley. Drain and stir through the Cheese Sauce with the tuna and parsley (Step 3 above).

Cook's tips
- You will need to cook ⅔ cup raw rice to make 2 cups cooked rice for this recipe.
- To make ahead and freeze for later, cover the dish well with plastic wrap and then foil, or in individual portions in airtight containers, and label. It will keep for up to 2 months in the freezer this way. Thaw in the refrigerator before reheating.

Pan-fried fish

Serves 4 Preparation time: 5 minutes Cooking time: 4–10 minutes
Gluten-free Carbohydrate 24g per adult serving, 12g per child serving

It's important to eat fish (fresh or canned) two or three times a week. But children (and some adults) often worry about bones in fresh fish. Remember that the tail end of a fillet has fewer, if any, bones and is a good option—and of course cutlets usually don't have any fine bones at all, just the larger backbone. Allow about 5¹/₄oz for each adult and 3oz for children.

4 fish fillets or cutlets
freshly ground black pepper, to
    taste
1 tsp olive or canola oil
lettuce, avocado, cucumber and red
    pepper salad, to serve
Sweet Potato Mash (see recipe
    page 170), to serve
lemon wedges, to serve

1 Season the fish with pepper. Heat the oil in a non-stick frying pan over medium–high heat until hot, swirling to coat the base. Add the fish and cook, turning halfway through cooking time, for 4–10 minutes (depending on the thickness of the fillets or cutlets) or until just cooked and the fish flakes when tested with a fork.
2 Serve immediately accompanied by the salad, Sweet Potato Mash and lemon wedges.

Shopping tip
For pan-frying, choose salmon fillets or cutlets, or tuna, flathead, snapper or bream fillets.

Baked crispy fish pieces

Serves 4 Preparation time: 10 minutes Cooking time: 10 minutes
Carbohydrate 17g per adult serving, 8g per child serving (excluding accompaniments)

Children love fish sticks, and so do parents as it's an easy meal to prepare and a great way to get kids eating more fish. But all too often the commercial brands are high in saturated fat and salt. Here we show you how to get all the benefits of crispy fish pieces prepared in the healthiest way possible and on the table in 20 minutes.

2 tbsp plain flour

freshly ground black pepper, to taste

1 egg, lightly whisked

2 tbsp reduced fat milk

1 cup firmly packed breadcrumbs (from day-old multigrain bread), toasted (see Cook's Tip below)

1/2 cup finely shredded parmesan (optional)

1lb boned skinless white fish fillets

olive oil cooking spray

Hummus or Guacamole (see recipes page 169), to serve

lettuce, cucumber and pepper salad, to serve

1 Preheat oven to 425°F and line an oven tray with parchment paper.

2 Spread the flour on a plate and season with pepper. Use a fork to whisk together the egg and milk in a shallow bowl. Combine the breadcrumbs and parmesan, if using, and spread on a plate.

3 Cut each fish fillet into manageable portions. Lightly dust the fish pieces with flour. Dip into the egg mixture, allowing any excess to drip off, and then coat well in the breadcrumb mixture, pressing the crumbs firmly so they stick. Place the coated fish pieces on the lined tray.

4 Lightly spray both sides of the fish pieces with the olive oil. Bake for 10 minutes or until golden, crisp and just cooked through, turning the pieces over halfway through cooking time.

5 Serve immediately accompanied by the Hummus or Guacamole and the salad.

Cook's tip
To toast breadcrumbs, spread crumbs on an oven tray and bake in an oven preheated to 350°F for 5–8 minutes or until golden. Cool on the tray.

Salmon cakes with lemon sauce

Serves 4 (makes 8) Preparation time: 20 minutes Chilling time: 30 minutes Cooking time: 25 minutes
Carbohydrate 15g per salmon cake (excluding sauce)

The trick to lowering the GI in good old-fashioned salmon or tuna cakes is to replace the potato with mashed cannellini beans—it's amazing, but no one will notice the difference. Actually, that's not quite true, they'll say it's creamier! You don't have to say why.

2 x 14oz cans cannellini beans, drained and rinsed

2 x 7oz cans red or pink salmon, drained, skin discarded, flesh coarsely flaked

2 eggs, lightly whisked

5 spring (green) onions, chopped

2 tbsp chopped chives

1 tsp finely grated lemon rind

freshly ground black pepper, to taste

1$\frac{1}{3}$ cups firmly packed breadcrumbs (from day-old multigrain or sourdough bread)

olive oil cooking spray

steamed, boiled or microwaved corn cobs and peas, to serve

lemon wedges, to serve

LEMON SAUCE

$\frac{1}{2}$ cup low fat plain yogurt

4 tsp baby capers, rinsed, chopped

3 tsp fresh lemon juice

1 Preheat oven to 400°F. Line an oven tray with parchment paper.
2 Place the beans in a medium-sized bowl and mash well with a fork or potato masher until creamy. Add the salmon, eggs, spring onions, chives and lemon rind and mix until well combined. Season with pepper.
3 Shape the mixture into 8 even-sized patties (children love to help here). Spread the breadcrumbs on a plate. Coat the patties with the breadcrumbs then place them on the lined tray and chill in the refrigerator for 30 minutes so that they will hold their shape during cooking.
4 Spray the salmon cakes lightly with olive oil on both sides. Bake for 25 minutes or until golden and thoroughly warmed through, turning them halfway through the cooking time so that they are crisp on both sides.
5 Meanwhile, to make the Lemon Sauce, combine the yogurt, capers and lemon juice and mix well. Cover and place in the refrigerator until required.
6 Serve the warm Salmon Cakes with the Lemon Sauce, corn, peas and lemon wedges.

VARIATION

Tuna cakes Carbohydrate 15g per tuna cake

14oz can tuna in springwater, drained, flaked

Make the recipe in the same way, replacing the salmon with tuna in Step 2.

Cook's tips

- Replace the canned salmon with 10$\frac{1}{2}$oz cooked fresh Atlantic salmon if you prefer.
- To reheat cooked salmon cakes, place on a tray lined with parchment paper then in an oven preheated to 350°F for 15–20 minutes or until heated through.
- To make ahead of time, prepare salmon cakes to the end of Step 3 or 4. Store for up to 2 days in an airtight container in the refrigerator.
- To freeze cooled, cooked salmon cakes for up to a month, cover in plastic wrap and seal in a freezer bag. Thaw in the refrigerator and reheat as above.

Macaroni and cheese

Serves 4 Preparation time: 15 minutes Cooking time: 40 minutes
Carbohydrate 66g per adult serving, 33g per child serving

This version of the family favorite Macaroni and Cheese is a complete meal in itself when the vegetables are included in the recipe. If you want to serve even more vegetables, add a crispy green salad with a vinaigrette dressing.

6^1/$_2$oz good-quality dried macaroni pasta (or your favorite short pasta shape)

1 brown onion, finely chopped

^{1}/$_2$ cup water

1 medium carrot, peeled, diced

1 small head broccoli (about 9oz), cut into small florets

1 cup frozen peas

1 quantity Cheese Sauce (see recipe page 172)

^{1}/$_2$ tsp Dijon mustard

^{1}/$_2$ cup coarsely grated reduced fat cheddar cheese

3^1/$_2$oz sliced lean ham, coarsely chopped

freshly ground black pepper, to taste

1 cup firmly packed breadcrumbs (from day-old multigrain or sourdough bread)

1 tbsp finely chopped flat-leaf (Italian) parsley (optional)

olive oil cooking spray

1 Preheat oven to 400°F.

2 Cook the macaroni in a large saucepan of boiling water following the packet instructions, or until al dente. Drain.

3 Meanwhile, combine the onion and ¼ cup of the water in a medium saucepan and cook, covered, stirring occasionally, for 8–10 minutes or until the onion is soft. Add the carrot, broccoli and remaining ¼ cup water, cover and cook, stirring occasionally, for 5 minutes or until the broccoli is tender-crisp. Stir in the peas and cook for a further 2 minutes. Remove from the heat and set aside.

4 Combine the Cheese Sauce, mustard and cheese in a medium-sized bowl. Add the ham and cooked macaroni and stir to combine. Add the vegetables and stir gently to combine evenly. Season with pepper.

5 Spoon into a 6 cup ovenproof dish and spread evenly. Combine the breadcrumbs and parsley, if using, and sprinkle over the pasta mixture. Spray lightly with the olive oil and bake for 20 minutes or until heated through and the topping is golden and crisp. Serve warm.

Cook's tips

- To make the day before, prepare to the end of Step 4 and spoon into baking dish. Cover the dish with plastic wrap and keep in the refrigerator. Continue the recipe from Step 5 when ready to serve.
- Store leftovers covered with plastic wrap or in an airtight container in the refrigerator. To reheat, cover the dish with foil and place in an oven preheated to 325°F for 15–20 minutes or until heated through.
- Freeze for up to 2 months in the dish covered well with plastic wrap and then foil or in individual portions in airtight containers. Thaw in the refrigerator and reheat as described above.

Soy and sesame marinated chicken drumsticks

Serves 4 Preparation time: 10 minutes Cooking time: 45–50 minutes
Carbohydrate 3g per drumstick (excluding accompaniments)

These drumsticks are also great to take in the lunch box. Just pack in an airtight container and transport in an insulated bag with an icepack.

2 tbsp salt-reduced soy sauce
1 tsp canola or vegetable oil
1 tsp sesame oil
2 tsp pure floral honey
3/4in piece ginger, finely grated
2 garlic cloves, crushed
4 chicken drumsticks
1 cup basmati, or other low GI rice, cooked following packet directions, to serve
steamed, boiled or microwaved corn on the cob and broccoli florets, to serve

1 Preheat oven to 425°F.
2 Combine the soy sauce, canola and sesame oils, honey, ginger and garlic in a small bowl and mix well.
3 Place the drumsticks in a small ovenproof dish (just large enough to hold them in a single layer), pour the marinade over, and turn to coat. Bake for 45–50 minutes, basting the drumsticks with the juices occasionally, or until browned and cooked through. Serve accompanied by the rice, corn and broccoli.

Cook's tip
To make ahead, combine the drumsticks with the marinade and store, covered, in the refrigerator for up to a day before cooking.

Thai chicken meatballs

Serves 4 Preparation time: 20 minutes Cooking time: 20 minutes
Carbohydrate 1g per meatball (excluding accompaniments)

These chicken meatballs are very versatile—serve them for dinner, as a snack or in a clear chicken soup with the mung bean noodles. The recipe makes 32 meatballs which is more than enough for a main meal. You'll find you have lots of helpers when rolling them. You can also make smaller meatballs (they'll only need about 10 minutes in the oven) and serve them as finger food when entertaining.

12oz ground chicken

1/4 cup unprocessed oat bran

1 small carrot, coarsely grated

1/2 small red pepper, deseeded, finely diced (optional)

2 spring (green) onions, finely chopped

2 tbsp finely chopped cilantro leaves

1 garlic clove, crushed

3 tsp salt-reduced soy sauce

2 tsp sweet chili sauce

canola oil cooking spray

7oz mung bean noodles, prepared following packet instructions, to serve

stir-fried Asian greens, to serve

sweet chili sauce, extra, to serve

1 Preheat oven to 400°F and line an oven tray with parchment paper.

2 Combine the ground chicken, oat bran, carrot, pepper (if using), spring onions, cilantro, garlic, soy sauce and sweet chili sauce. Use your hands to mix until evenly combined.

3 With damp hands, roll the mixture into walnut-sized balls and place on the lined oven tray. Spray the meatballs lightly with the canola oil and bake for 20 minutes or until lightly golden and cooked through.

4 Serve warm accompanied by the mung bean noodles, Asian greens and the extra sweet chili sauce for dipping.

Cook's tip

You can make the meatballs the day before and store in an airtight container in the refrigerator. To reheat, place on an oven tray lined with parchment paper in an oven preheated to 350°F for 10 minutes, or until heated through.

Chicken and pumpkin soup with quinoa

Serves 6 Preparation time: 15 minutes Cooking time: 30–35 minutes
Gluten-free Carbohydrate 25g per serving

When a warm and comforting soup is all that's needed, this is the perfect meal in a bowl. Quinoa (pronounced keen-wa) *is a small, round, quick-cooking grain that's an excellent source of low GI carbs, fiber and complete protein, as well as being rich in B vitamins and minerals. Health food stores, organic shops and larger supermarkets are where you'll find it. Introduce it to your family in tasty recipes like this chicken soup.*

1 small brown onion, finely chopped

1 leek (pale section only), cleaned, halved lengthwise, thinly sliced

2 medium carrots, scrubbed, diced

1 celery stick, diced

2 garlic cloves, crushed

2 tsp ground cumin

$2^1/2$ cups water

4 cups salt-reduced chicken stock

18oz chicken breast or tenderloin fillets, trimmed

$3/4$ cup quinoa, rinsed

14oz pumpkin, peeled, deseeded, cut into $1/2$in pieces

freshly ground black pepper, to taste

2 tbsp chopped flat-leaf (Italian) parsley

1 Combine the onion, leek, carrots, celery, garlic, cumin and $1/2$ cup water in a medium saucepan. Cover and cook over medium heat, stirring occasionally, for 10 minutes or until the onion is tender.

2 Add the remaining 2 cups water, the chicken stock and the chicken. Bring to a simmer over medium heat. Reduce heat to low and cook, very gently, for a further 2–5 minutes or until the chicken is just tender. Remove the chicken from the soup with a slotted spoon and set aside.

3 Add the quinoa to the soup. Bring back to a simmer over high heat then reduce heat to medium and simmer for 10 minutes. Add the pumpkin and simmer for a further 5 minutes or until the pumpkin and quinoa are tender.

4 Meanwhile, use 2 forks or your fingers to shred the chicken. Add the chicken to the soup and heat through. Taste, season with pepper and serve immediately sprinkled with the parsley.

Cook's tip
Quinoa is cooked when the grain appears translucent and the "germ ring" is visible.

Easy fried rice

Serves 4 Preparation time: 15 minutes Cooking time: 10–15 minutes
Gluten-free (if made with gluten-free soy sauce) Carbohydrate 73g per adult serving, 37g per child serving

This is a great, all-in-one meal that encourages children to eat a variety of vegetables. It also makes a satisfying (and very popular) after-school snack. Adapt the ingredients to suit your child's preferred vegetables and meat—try substituting peas, carrot, zucchini, bean sprouts, ham, bacon or pork; the options are endless. Best of all, this is also a great one to put in the lunch box. Transport in an airtight container in an insulated bag with an icepack.

2 eggs

2 tsp water

4 tsp canola or peanut oil

10$\frac{1}{2}$oz trimmed chicken fillets (breast, tenderloin or thigh), cut into bite-sized pieces

1 small red pepper, halved lengthways, deseeded, thinly sliced

2 small corn cobs, kernels removed (or 1 punnet baby corn, cut into $\frac{1}{2}$in pieces)

1 head broccoli (about 10$\frac{1}{2}$oz), cut into small florets

4 spring (green) onions, thinly sliced

1 garlic clove, crushed

$\frac{1}{2}$ tsp finely grated fresh ginger

$\frac{1}{4}$ cup water, extra

3 cups cold cooked low GI rice

1$\frac{1}{2}$ tbsp salt-reduced soy sauce

$\frac{1}{2}$ Lebanese cucumber, diced

1 Use a fork to whisk together the eggs and water in a small bowl. Heat 1 teaspoon of the oil in a large non-stick wok or a non-stick frying pan over high heat until hot, swirling to coat the surface. Add the egg mixture and swirl again to make an omelette. Cook for 30 seconds or until the egg is just set. Roll the omelette up and transfer to a plate. Slice into thin strips and set aside.

2 Toss chicken with 1 teaspoon of the remaining oil. Reheat the wok until hot, add the chicken and stir-fry for 2–3 minutes or until just cooked through. Remove from wok and set aside.

3 Add the remaining 2 teaspoons of oil, pepper, corn, broccoli, spring onions, garlic and ginger to the wok and stir-fry over medium–high heat for 2 minutes, tossing frequently. Add the extra $\frac{1}{4}$ cup water and cook until the water evaporates and the vegetables are tender-crisp.

4 Add the chicken, rice and soy sauce and toss until heated through. Serve topped with the egg strips and cucumber.

Cook's tips
• You will need 1 cup uncooked rice to make 3 cups cooked rice.
• Make the fried rice a day ahead and store in an airtight container in the refrigerator. Reheat in a non-stick wok or frying pan over medium heat until warmed through.

Honey and oregano roasted leg of lamb
with roasted vegetables

Serves 6 (with leftovers for 4) Preparation time: 10 minutes Cooking time: 50–60 minutes Resting time: 15 minutes
Gluten-free Carbohydrate 40g per serving (including Roasted Vegetables)

Roast dinners are a real family affair. And although they take a little longer to cook, you can get on with other chores, supervise homework or catch up on your emails while dinner is in the oven.

1 cup water
3lb 6oz leg of lamb, trimmed of all
  visible fat
2 large garlic cloves, sliced
8 sprigs oregano, each halved
2 tbsp pure floral honey
4 tsp Dijon mustard
2 tsp lemon juice
1 quantity Roasted Vegetables
  (without Hummus) (see recipe
  page 171), to serve
steamed, boiled or microwaved
  green beans

1 Preheat oven to 400°F. Place a rack in a roasting pan and add the water to the pan.
2 Use a small sharp knife to cut slits all over the surface of the lamb. Poke the garlic slices and sprigs of oregano into the slits.
3 Place the lamb on the rack in the roasting pan and roast for 30 minutes.
4 Combine the honey, mustard and lemon juice. Brush over the lamb and return to the oven for a further 20 minutes for medium or 30 minutes for well-done. Remove lamb from oven, cover loosely with foil and set aside in a warm place for 15 minutes to rest.
5 Carve the lamb and serve accompanied by the Roasted Vegetables and beans.

Cook's tip
Add the Roasted Vegetables to the oven after the lamb has been roasting for 15 minutes. They will finish cooking while the lamb is resting.

Barbecued satay lamb kebabs

Serves 4 Preparation time: 15 minutes Marinating time: 30 minutes Cooking time: 10 minutes
Carbohydrate 48g per serving (2 skewers)

We have made these kebabs with onion wedges, but they are just as delicious with pieces of red pepper threaded onto the skewers with the lamb. Or use both onion and pepper to make them more substantial. If you are using bamboo skewers, soak them in water for 30 minutes beforehand to prevent them from burning on the barbecue.

14oz lamb fillets, cut into 1in pieces

1 tsp olive or canola oil

1 small red onion, cut into thin wedges

1¹/₂ tbsp water

1 cup basmati or other low GI rice, cooked following packet directions, to serve

steamed, boiled or microwaved snow peas and sugar snap peas or Corn Cakes (see recipe page 167), to serve

SATAY MARINADE

2 tbsp salt-reduced soy sauce

1 tbsp pure floral honey

1 tbsp smooth peanut butter

1 garlic clove, crushed

1 To make the Satay Marinade, place the soy sauce, honey, peanut butter and garlic in a medium bowl and use a fork to combine. Add the lamb and toss to coat in the marinade. Cover and place in the refrigerator for at least 30 minutes.

2 Brush a barbecue plate or grill with the oil and preheat on medium.

3 Remove the lamb from the marinade, reserving the mixture. Alternately thread the lamb and onion wedges onto 8 short skewers.

4 Place the skewers on the preheated barbecue and cook, turning once, for 5 minutes for medium, or until cooked to your liking. Transfer the skewers to a plate and cover loosely with foil. Set aside in a warm place for 5 minutes to rest.

5 Meanwhile, place the reserved marinade in a small saucepan. Stir in the water and bring to a simmer then cook for 2 minutes to make a satay sauce.

6 Serve lamb skewers accompanied by the rice, satay sauce, and the sugar snap and snow peas or Corn Cakes.

Cook's tip
You can marinate the lamb and thread onto the skewers with the onion the day before then store in an airtight container in the refrigerator. Stand at room temperature for 15 minutes before cooking.

Hokkien noodles with pork, vegetables and egg

Serves 4 Preparation time: 15 minutes Cooking time: 15 minutes
Carbohydrate 76g per adult serving, 38g per child serving

Any combination of vegetables can be used in this stir-fry. Try baby corn or corn kernels, carrot sticks or halved or quartered baby carrots, shredded or baby spinach, zucchini sticks, sugar snap peas, shredded cabbage or gai lan (Chinese broccoli) cut into short lengths. Remember to add them to the stir-fry depending on their cooking times—add the more dense vegetables first.

14oz pork fillet, thinly sliced

1 garlic clove, crushed

4 tsp canola or peanut oil

14oz fresh thin hokkien noodles (see Shopping Tip below)

2 eggs, lightly whisked

1 brown onion, cut into thin wedges

5$\frac{1}{4}$oz mushrooms, stems trimmed, sliced

1 bunch baby bok choy, leaves separated and washed, stems cut into $\frac{3}{4}$in lengths

1 head broccoli (about 9oz), cut into small florets

1 red pepper, deseeded, cut into thin strips

1in piece ginger, finely grated

4 tsp oyster sauce

1$\frac{1}{2}$ tbsp salt-reduced soy sauce

$\frac{1}{4}$ cup water

1 Combine the pork, garlic and half the oil. Set aside.

2 Prepare the hokkien noodles following packet directions. Set aside.

3 Add 1 teaspoon of the remaining oil to a wok and heat on high until hot. Add the eggs and tilt so they coat the sides and form an omelette. Cook for 30 seconds or until just set. Remove from the pan, roll up and cut into strips. Set aside.

4 Reheat the wok over high heat. Add half the pork and stir-fry for 1–2 minutes or until just cooked through. Transfer to a plate then repeat with the remaining pork.

5 Add the remaining oil to the wok and reheat until hot. Add the onion and stir-fry for 2 minutes. Add the mushrooms and stir-fry for 1–2 minutes or until starting to soften. Add the bok choy stems, broccoli, pepper and ginger and stir-fry for 1 minute. Add the bok choy leaves, oyster sauce, soy sauce and water, cover the wok and cook, tossing occasionally, for a further 2 minutes or until the vegetables are tender-crisp.

6 Return the pork to the wok with the noodles and toss to combine and heat through. Serve immediately topped with the egg strips.

VARIATIONS

Hokkien noodles with chicken and vegetables

Carbohydrate 76g per adult serving, 38g per child serving

14oz trimmed chicken tenderloins or fillets

Cut the chicken across the grain into thin strips. Follow the cooking instructions above, replacing the pork with chicken.

Hokkien noodles with shrimp and vegetables

Carbohydrate 76g per adult serving, 38g per child serving

20 (18oz) medium king shrimp, peeled with tails left intact and deveined

Follow the cooking directions above, replacing the pork with the shrimp.

Shopping tip
You'll find fresh hokkien noodles in the supermarket, either in the Asian section in long-life packets or in the refrigerated section.

Lamb cutlets with spiced pilaf

Serves 6 Preparation time: 15 minutes Marinating time: 1 hour Cooking time: 30–35 minutes
Gluten-free Carbohydrate 30g per serving

This recipe is perfect for when you're entertaining family and friends as it's an easy one to extend by doubling quantities to feed a crowd. Try cooking the cutlets on the grill for a change.

$1^1/_2$ tbsp lemon juice

$^1/_2$ tsp olive oil

$1^1/_2$ tsp ground cumin

1 tsp paprika

12 french-trimmed lamb cutlets

steamed, boiled or microwaved
   patty pan squash and green
   beans, to serve

7oz low fat plain yogurt,
   to serve

lemon wedges, to serve

SPICED PILAF

2 tsp olive oil

1 brown onion, finely chopped

1 garlic clove, crushed

3 cardamom pods, crushed

$^3/_4$ tsp ground cinnamon

6 whole cloves

pinch saffron threads

$^3/_4$ cup basmati rice, rinsed and
   drained

$1^1/_2$ cups salt-reduced chicken stock

$10^1/_2$oz can chickpeas, drained and
   rinsed

2 tbsp chopped cilantro leaves

1 Combine the lemon juice, oil, cumin and paprika in a small bowl. Pour mixture over the lamb cutlets and rub in well to coat. Cover and place the lamb in the refrigerator for at least 1 hour to marinate (if time permits).

2 To make the Spiced Pilaf, place the oil and onion in a medium-sized saucepan and cook onion over medium heat, stirring frequently, for 5–8 minutes or until onion is soft. Add the garlic, cardamom pods, cinnamon, cloves and saffron and cook for a further minute or until aromatic. Add the rice and stir for 1 minute or until coated with the spice mixture and starting to stick to the base of the pan. Pour in chicken stock and bring to a simmer over high heat. Reduce heat to the lowest possible setting, cover and cook gently for 15 minutes, or until all the liquid has been absorbed. Remove from the heat. Set aside for 5 minutes then use a fork to stir the chickpeas through the rice.

3 Meanwhile, heat a large chargrill or non-stick frying pan over medium–high heat. Add the lamb cutlets and cook for 2 minutes each side for medium or until cooked to your liking. Transfer to a plate, cover loosely with foil and set aside in a warm place for 5 minutes to rest.

4 To serve, use a fork to stir the cilantro through the pilaf. Serve the cutlets accompanied by the pilaf, squash, beans, yogurt and lemon wedges.

Cook's tip
You can marinate the cutlets and make the Spiced Pilaf the day before you need them, then store in separate airtight containers in the refrigerator.

Lamb patties with bulgur

Serves 4 Soaking time: 20 minutes Preparation time: 20 minutes Cooking time: 8–10 minutes
Carbohydrate 7g per patty (excluding accompaniments)

If your local supermarket doesn't stock ground lamb, ask your butcher to grind some lean lamb leg or shoulder meat for you. Alternatively, buy 18oz lean lamb leg or shoulder, trim the fat and cut into cubes. Grind with a grinding attachment or process in batches in a food processor until very finely chopped.

$1/4$ cup bulgur

$1/3$ cup unprocessed oat bran

2 tbsp reduced fat milk

14oz lean ground lamb

1 egg white, lightly whisked

1 medium zucchini, coarsely grated

1 small brown onion, coarsely grated

2 tbsp chopped mint

1 small garlic clove, crushed

1 tsp ground cumin

freshly ground black pepper, to taste

1 tsp olive oil

Sweet Potato Mash (see recipe page 170), to serve

mixed salad, to serve

1 Place the bulgur in a small bowl. Cover with cold water and set aside to soak for 20 minutes. Drain and then use your hands to press out any excess water.

2 Transfer the bulgur to a large bowl. Add the oat bran and milk and stir to combine. Add the ground lamb, egg white, zucchini, onion, mint, garlic, cumin and pepper. Use your hands to mix well until evenly combined. Shape the mixture into 12 patties about $2^1/2$in wide and $3/4$in thick.

3 Heat the olive oil in a large non-stick frying pan over medium heat until hot, swirling to coat the base. Add the patties and cook for 4–5 minutes each side or until golden and cooked through. Serve accompanied by the Sweet Potato Mash and salad.

Cook's tip
You can cook the patties up to 2 days ahead and store in an airtight container in the refrigerator. Reheat in a non-stick frying pan over medium–low heat for 3 minutes each side or until warmed through.

Italian meatballs with spaghetti

Serves 4 Preparation time: 20 minutes Cooking time: 10 minutes
Carbohydrate 70g per adult serving, 35g per child serving

You just haven't eaten meatballs until you've tried these, one of Anneka's specialties. The secret is the texture. It's one of those recipes that becomes a family favorite (it has for our families) and puts a smile on every face at the end of the day. It also gives children with homework or assignments to complete all the energy they need for that extra hour or three of study.

14oz lean ground beef

¾ cup firmly packed breadcrumbs (from day-old multigrain or sourdough bread)

¼ cup reduced fat milk

1 small brown onion, coarsely grated

¼ cup roughly chopped flat-leaf (Italian) parsley or basil leaves

¼ cup parmesan, finely grated, plus extra, to serve

1 garlic clove, crushed

½ tsp chili flakes (optional)

freshly ground black pepper, to taste

1 quantity Easy Tomato Sauce (see recipe page 173)

½ cup salt-reduced beef or chicken stock

6½oz good-quality dried spaghetti, cooked until al dente, to serve

garden salad with mixed leaves, tomato wedges, chopped cucumber and pepper tossed in a vinaigrette dressing, to serve

1 Combine the ground beef, breadcrumbs, milk, onion, parsley, parmesan, garlic, chili flakes (if using) and pepper in a medium-sized bowl and use your hands to mix well until evenly combined. Roll the mixture into walnut-sized balls. Place on a plate or tray, cover and set aside.

2 Combine the Easy Tomato Sauce and stock in a large frying pan and bring to a simmer over high heat. Add the meatballs in a single layer, reduce heat to low–medium, cover and simmer gently, turning the meatballs halfway through cooking, for 8 minutes or until just cooked through.

3 Season with pepper. Serve over the spaghetti, sprinkle with the extra grated parmesan and serve accompanied by the green salad.

VARIATION

Meatballs in tomato sauce with couscous

Carbohydrate 79g per adult serving, 40g per child serving

1 tsp ground cumin

1 tsp paprika (optional)

¼ cup roughly chopped cilantro, flat-leaf (Italian) parsley or mint leaves

1 cup good-quality couscous, prepared following packet instructions, to serve

steamed, boiled or microwaved sliced zucchini and broccoli florets or a green salad, to serve

Add the cumin and paprika (if using) in Step 1, replacing the onion, parsley or basil, parmesan, garlic and chili, and continue following the basic method. Stir the cilantro through the sauce with the pepper. Omit the spaghetti and serve with the couscous, zucchini and broccoli, or green salad.

Cook's tip
You can prepare and cook the meatballs and sauce up to 2 days before serving. Keep in an airtight container in the refrigerator until ready to reheat.

Beef stir-fry with noodles, corn and snow peas

Serves 4 Preparation time: 20 minutes Cooking time: 15 minutes
Carbohydrate 48g per adult serving, 24g per child serving

Quick and easy noodle stir-fries seem to appeal to everyone—even children who loudly proclaim that they hate vegetables. The trick is to cook in a hot wok, stir-fry the meat in batches and not overcook the vegetables. Crisp is the name of the stir-fry game. Follow our well-tested method here and your family will think it's from their favorite Asian takeout.

4 tsp Chinese rice wine (see Shopping Tip below)

4 tsp canola or peanut oil

1 tsp cornflour

14oz trimmed lean beef rump steak (about $^1/_2$in thick), cut across the grain into thin strips

1 bunch gai lan (Chinese broccoli), ends trimmed

5$^1/_2$oz dried thin egg noodles

1in piece ginger, finely grated

4$^1/_2$oz baby corn, halved lengthwise

5$^1/_4$oz snow peas, topped

2 tbsp salt-reduced soy sauce

2 tsp sambal oelek (optional)

2 tbsp water

$^1/_2$ tsp sesame oil

4 spring (green) onions, thinly sliced diagonally

1 Combine the rice wine, 2 teaspoons of the oil and the cornflour in a medium-sized bowl and mix until smooth. Add the steak and mix well to coat. Cover and set aside to marinate while preparing the other ingredients.

2 Cut the stems of the gai lan into short lengths and shred the leaves.

3 Cook the noodles in a large saucepan of boiling water following the packet instructions until tender. Drain, cover to keep warm and set aside.

4 Heat a non-stick wok on high until it's very hot. Add half the steak to the hot wok and stir-fry for 30–60 seconds or until sealed. Use a slotted spoon to transfer the cooked meat to a plate. Repeat with the remaining steak.

5 Add the remaining 2 teaspoons of oil to the wok and reheat until hot. Add the gai lan stems and stir-fry for 1 minute. Add the ginger and corn and stir-fry for 1 minute or until aromatic. Add the snow peas, gai lan leaves, soy sauce, sambal oelek (if using), water and sesame oil and cook for 2 minutes, tossing occasionally, until the snow peas are bright green and the vegetables are tender-crisp.

6 Return the meat to the wok with the noodles and spring onions, toss gently to combine and heat through. Serve immediately.

Shopping tip
Chinese rice wine is also known as shaoxing (or shao hsing). You will find it in Asian food stores and larger supermarkets. Substitute dry sherry if needed.

Sang choy bau

Serves 4 Preparation time: 15 minutes Cooking time: 15 minutes
Carbohydrate 22g per adult serving, 11g per child serving

This is a great dish to place in the center of the table and allow everyone to fill their own lettuce cups, though you may have to keep a watchful eye to make sure everyone gets a fair share—some people seem to be able to get much more on the serving spoon than others!

$3^{1}/_{2}$oz mung bean noodles

1 tsp peanut oil

1 brown onion, finely chopped

1in piece ginger, finely grated

1 garlic clove, crushed

14oz lean ground pork

$^{2}/_{3}$ cup canned sliced water chestnuts, drained, finely chopped

4 spring (green) onions, thinly sliced diagonally

4 tsp oyster sauce

4 tsp salt-reduced soy sauce

2 tbsp chopped cilantro leaves (optional)

8 large iceberg lettuce leaves, trimmed to form large "cups"

1 Lebanese cucumber, halved lengthwise, thinly sliced diagonally

1 cup bean sprouts

1 Prepare the noodles following the packet instructions. Drain and cut the noodles into short lengths with kitchen scissors. Set aside.

2 Place the peanut oil and onion in a non-stick wok or large non-stick frying pan and cook over medium heat, stirring occasionally, for 5–8 minutes or until onion is soft. Add the ginger and garlic and cook for 1 more minute or until aromatic.

3 Increase the heat to high, add the ground pork to the wok and cook, breaking up with the back of a wooden spoon, for 5 minutes or until just cooked through. Add the drained noodles, water chestnuts, spring onions, oyster sauce, soy sauce and cilantro (if using) and stir until evenly combined and heated through. Serve immediately in lettuce cups and topped with the cucumber and bean sprouts.

VARIATIONS

Veal and pork sang choy bau
Carbohydrate 22g per adult serving, 11g per child serving

14oz lean ground veal and pork

Follow the cooking instructions above, replacing the ground pork with ground veal and pork.

Chicken sang choy bau
Carbohydrate 22g per adult serving, 11g per child serving

14oz lean ground chicken

Follow the cooking instructions above, replacing the ground pork with ground chicken.

Vegetarian tacos

Serves 6 Preparation time: 15 minutes Cooking time: 10 minutes
Vegetarian and Gluten-free Carbohydrate 39g per serving (2 tacos)

There's nothing like tacos to get the family to feast on those nutrition power packs—legumes. To add a little heat to the occasion, add 1 chopped red chili to the tomato sauce with the red kidney beans and paprika.

1 quantity Easy Tomato Sauce
   (see recipe page 173)
2 x 10$\frac{1}{2}$oz cans red kidney beans,
   drained and rinsed
1 tsp mild paprika
freshly ground black pepper,
   to taste
12 taco shells
$\frac{1}{2}$ iceberg lettuce, shredded
2 carrots, scrubbed, coarsely grated
1$\frac{1}{2}$ cups coarsely grated reduced
   fat cheddar cheese
1$\frac{1}{2}$ quantities Guacamole (see
   recipe page 169)

1 Place the Easy Tomato Sauce in a medium saucepan. Add the red kidney beans and paprika and bring to a simmer over medium heat. Simmer for 10 minutes or until thick. Taste and season with pepper.
2 Transfer the red kidney bean mixture to a serving bowl. Place on the table with the taco shells, lettuce, carrots, cheese and Guacamole for everyone to assemble their own tacos.

Cook's tip

You can make the red kidney bean mixture a day or two ahead and store in an airtight container in the refrigerator. Reheat in a saucepan over medium heat, stirring occasionally, until simmering.

Spaghetti bolognese

Serves 6 Preparation time: 15 minutes Cooking time: 50–65 minutes
Carbohydrate 46g per serving

This is a very adaptable recipe—substitute your family's favorite vegetables for the zucchini and carrot if you wish. And you can make the sauce up to 3 days ahead if stored in the refrigerator.

5^1/$_4$oz button mushrooms

1 brown onion, finely chopped

2 garlic cloves, crushed

1^1/$_4$ cups water

10^1/$_2$oz lean ground beef

1 zucchini, finely grated

1 carrot, scrubbed, finely grated

^{1}/$_3$ cup split red lentils

1^1/$_2$lb bottle passata (see Shopping Tip below)

2 tbsp no-added-salt tomato paste

1 tsp dried oregano or mixed herbs

10oz good-quality dried spaghetti

^{1}/$_4$ cup chopped flat-leaf (Italian) parsley or basil (optional)

freshly ground black pepper, to taste

^{1}/$_2$ cup finely shredded parmesan or ^{1}/$_2$ cup reduced fat cheddar cheese, to serve (optional)

1 Combine the mushrooms, onion, garlic and ^{1}/$_4$ cup of the water in a large saucepan and cook, over medium heat, covered and stirring occasionally, for 8–10 minutes or until tender. Remove the lid and cook until the liquid evaporates.

2 Increase the heat to high and add the beef. Cook, breaking up with the back of a wooden spoon, for 2–3 minutes or until browned.

3 Add the zucchini, carrot, lentils, passata, tomato paste, oregano or mixed herbs and remaining 1 cup water and bring to a boil. Reduce heat and simmer, stirring occasionally, for 40–50 minutes or until the lentils are tender and the sauce has thickened.

4 Meanwhile, cook the spaghetti in a large saucepan of boiling water following packet directions, or until al dente. Drain.

5 Stir parsley through the sauce, if using, taste and season with pepper. Serve over the pasta and sprinkle with cheese, if desired.

VARIATION

Squash and spinach lasagna

Serves 6 Preparation time: 25 minutes Cooking time: 1 hour and 25 minutes–1 hour 45 and minutes Carbohydrate 42g per serving

5^1/$_4$oz instant lasagna sheets

^{1}/$_2$ butternut squash, peeled, deseeded, cut into ^{1}/$_4$in slices

3oz baby spinach

1 quantity Cheese Sauce (see recipe page 172)

leafy green salad, to serve

1 Preheat oven to 350°F. Make the bolognese sauce following the above method. Omit the spaghetti and grated cheese. Add an extra ^{1}/$_2$ cup of water to the sauce.

2 Spread a third of the sauce over the base of a 7 x 12in ovenproof dish. Cover with a third of the lasagna sheets. Top with half the squash slices and then half the spinach.

3 Repeat layering with half the remaining bolognese sauce, half the lasagna sheets, the remaining squash and the remaining spinach. Top with the remaining bolognese sauce and lasagna sheets. Spread the Cheese Sauce evenly over the lasagna sheets to cover.

4 Bake for 35–40 minutes or until the top is golden and the lasagna sheets and squash are tender. Serve accompanied by the salad.

Shopping tip

You'll find passata, a tomato-based sauce or puree, in the pasta or pasta sauces section of your supermarket. If you can't get it, substitute with the equivalent amount of canned tomato puree.

Pearl barley risotto with squash and spinach

Serves 4 Preparation time: 15 minutes Cooking time: 1 hour and 15 minutes
Vegetarian Carbohydrate 55g per adult serving, 28g per child serving

This risotto is also great served at room temperature. To do so, remove the saucepan from the heat, cover it and set aside for 30–45 minutes or until cool. Then stir through the cilantro just before serving.

4 tsp olive oil

1 red onion, cut into thin wedges

2 garlic cloves, crushed

$1^1/_2$ tsp ground cumin

$1^1/_2$ tsp ground cilantro

1 tsp ground cinnamon

$^1/_2$ tsp mild paprika (optional)

$^1/_3$ cup pearl barley

$^1/_3$ cup yellow split peas

$2^1/_2$ cups salt-reduced chicken stock

2lb 4oz butternut squash (about 1 small), peeled, deseeded, cut into $^3/_4$in chunks

$3^1/_2$oz baby spinach leaves

freshly ground black pepper, to taste

$^1/_4$ cup roughly chopped cilantro or mint leaves (optional)

7oz low fat plain yogurt, to serve

steamed, boiled or microwaved yellow squash and green beans, to serve

1 Place the oil and onion in a large heavy-based saucepan and cook over medium heat, stirring occasionally, for 5–8 minutes or until soft. Add the garlic, cumin, cilantro, cinnamon and paprika (if using) and stir for 1 minute or until aromatic.

2 Add the pearl barley and yellow split peas and cook, stirring occasionally, for 2 minutes. Add the stock and bring to a boil over high heat. Reduce heat to low, cover and cook gently for 40 minutes.

3 Stir in the squash. Cover again and bring back to a boil over high heat. Reduce heat to low and cook, covered and stirring occasionally, for a further 18–20 minutes or until squash is tender and almost all the liquid has been absorbed. Stir through the spinach and cook for a further 1–2 minutes or until the spinach just wilts. Remove from heat, taste and season with pepper. Stir through the cilantro, if using, and serve accompanied by a dollop of yogurt, and the squash and beans.

Cook's tip

You can make this risotto a day or two ahead and store in an airtight container in the refrigerator. Reheat in a large saucepan over medium heat, stirring occasionally, until heated through. You may need to add a little water to the risotto while reheating it to reach the desired consistency.

easy pasta ideas

Pasta with squash sauce

Cook 1 chopped brown onion in a little olive oil in a large saucepan until tender. Add 2 chopped garlic cloves and cook for 1 minute. Peel, deseed and dice 2lb butternut squash (about $1/2$ large squash). Add to the saucepan and cook for 5 minutes, stirring frequently, or until starting to soften. Cover with salt-reduced vegetable or chicken stock. Simmer until the squash is very tender, adding a little water to keep the squash covered if necessary. Blend the squash and stock mixture, in batches if necessary, until smooth. Return to the saucepan and simmer until a thick soup consistency. Season well with freshly ground black pepper. Meanwhile, boil $11^1/4$oz short pasta shapes (such as macaroni) until al dente. Drain. Add to the squash sauce and toss to coat. Serve sprinkled with chopped parsley or chives and a sprinkling of nutmeg if desired. **Serves 4**

Speedy pasta with tomatoes and basil

Boil $11^1/4$oz short pasta (such as penne or shells) until al dente. Drain. Cook 1 clove of crushed garlic with 1 tablespoon of olive oil in a large saucepan until tender. Add $8^3/4$oz small cherry tomatoes and 5oz semi-dried tomatoes and cook for 2–3 minutes. Add the drained pasta and mix it well with the tomatoes and garlic. Remove the pan from the heat, add $3^1/2$oz buffalo mozzarella (torn into pieces), $1^1/2$ cups roughly chopped arugula, $1/3$ cup torn basil leaves and 1 teaspoon finely grated lemon zest. Season with freshly ground black pepper and serve immediately. **Serves 4**

desserts and sweet treats

"Treats are energy for storing away"

Sweets put a smile on everyone's face and can bring a family meal to a pleasant close. Naturally sweet fruits—fresh berries with honey yogurt, apples or bananas caramelized in a pan, stone fruit roasted under a grill or simply a fresh fruit salad with some low fat ice cream—make the perfect dessert.

Apple and pear crumble with maple syrup yogurt

Serves 6 Preparation time: 20 minutes Cooking time: 30–40 minutes
Vegetarian Carbohydrate 34g per serving (including yogurt)

Centering family desserts like this comforting crumble around fruit and low fat dairy products can make them a healthy and low GI addition to the meal. If there are any leftovers, try it for breakfast served at room temperature with a dollop of low fat plain or vanilla yogurt.

2 apples (such as Granny Smith,
 Golden Delicious or Royal Gala)
2 firm ripe pears (such as Williams
 or Packham)
2 tsp fresh lemon juice

CRUMBLE TOPPING
1/2 cup rolled barley (see Shopping
 Tip below)
1oz plain flour
1/2 tsp baking powder
1/2 tsp ground cinnamon
1oz canola or olive oil margarine
1 1/2 tbsp brown sugar
1/3 cup pecans,
 coarsely chopped

MAPLE SYRUP YOGURT
4 tsp pure maple syrup
7oz tub low fat vanilla yogurt

1 Preheat oven to 325°F.
2 Peel, quarter and core the apples and pears. Cut into thin slices, sprinkle with the lemon juice and toss to coat the fruit. Divide among 6 x 1/2 cup ovenproof dishes. Set aside.
3 To make the Crumble Topping, process half of the rolled barley in a food processor until finely ground and resembling flour. Transfer to a medium-sized bowl. Sift the plain flour, baking powder and cinnamon together into the bowl over the barley "flour." Add the margarine and use your fingertips to rub in until evenly combined. Stir in the brown sugar, pecans and the remaining rolled barley.
4 Sprinkle the Crumble Topping over the fruit in the dishes. Bake for 30–40 minutes or until the topping is golden and the fruit is tender when pierced by a skewer.
5 Meanwhile, to make the Maple Syrup Yogurt, stir the maple syrup through the yogurt. Cover and place in the refrigerator until required.
6 Serve the warm crumble accompanied by the Maple Syrup Yogurt.

Shopping tip
You can buy rolled barley in health food shops, organic stores and larger supermarkets. If unavailable, replace it with the same amount of rolled oats.

Cook's tip
You can make the crumble a day or two ahead, cover the dishes with plastic wrap and store in the refrigerator. Reheat at 325°F for 10–15 minutes or until heated through.

Fruit skewers with passion fruit yogurt dip

Serves 4 Preparation time: 15 minutes

Vegetarian and Gluten-free Carbohydrate 31g per adult serving, 16g per child serving (including dip)

You could also use 1oz of dried fruit, such as apricots or peaches, as part of your fruit selection if you wish.

Choose 4 portions of seasonal fresh fruit from:

1 pear, cored, cut into thin wedges

1 firm ripe banana, thickly sliced

1 apple (such as Royal Gala, Pink Lady or Golden Delicious), cored, cut into thin wedges

4^1/$_2$oz strawberries, hulled, halved if large

1 orange, peeled and segmented

1 large peach, deseeded, cut into thin wedges

2 large apricots, deseeded, cut into thin wedges

^{1}/$_2$ large ripe mango, flesh cut into chunks

PASSION FRUIT YOGURT DIP

7oz tub low fat vanilla yogurt

2 passion fruit, pulp removed

1 tsp pure floral honey, or to taste (optional)

1 To make the Passion Fruit Yogurt Dip, combine the yogurt and passion fruit pulp and stir well. Taste and sweeten with honey (if using). Place in a serving dish, cover and refrigerate until serving time.

2 Thread the fruit onto short skewers or toothpicks. Serve accompanied by the Passion Fruit Yogurt Dip for dipping.

VARIATION

Fruit skewers with chocolate fondue

Carbohydrate 47g per adult serving 24g per child serving

2^3/$_4$oz good-quality dark chocolate, chopped

2 tbsp light evaporated milk

^{1}/$_2$ tsp vanilla essence

Omit the Passion Fruit Yogurt Dip for this version. Prepare the fruit skewers as described above. To make the chocolate fondue dipping sauce, combine the chocolate, light evaporated milk and vanilla essence in a small saucepan. Stir over low heat until chocolate melts and the mixture is smooth. Pour into a bowl and serve immediately with the fruit skewers.

Frozen berry yogurt

Serves 6 Preparation time: 10 minutes Freezing time: 7 hours
Vegetarian and Gluten-free Carbohydrate 21g per serving

This frozen yogurt is easy to prepare. It makes about 2¹/₂ cups—plenty for 6 people. You can refreeze it in single serve containers in Step 3 rather than 1 large container if you prefer and have it on hand as an after-school snack.

9oz fresh or frozen mixed berries
3 x 7oz tubs low fat vanilla yogurt
2 egg whites
2 tbsp pure floral honey

Cook's tip
Make up to 2 weeks ahead and store in an airtight container in the freezer.

1 Place the berries and yogurt in a food processor and blend until smooth. Transfer to a medium-sized bowl and set aside.
2 Use electric beaters with a whisk attachment or a balloon whisk to whisk the egg whites in a clean, dry bowl until stiff peaks form. Add the honey a tablespoon at a time, whisking well after each addition until thick and glossy. Fold into the berry yogurt mixture until just combined.
3 Pour the mixture into an airtight container and place in the freezer for 4 hours or until frozen. Use a metal spoon to break the frozen yogurt into chunks. Blend again in a food processor until smooth. Return to the airtight container and refreeze for 3 hours or until frozen. Serve in scoops.

VARIATIONS
Frozen berry yogurt popsicles
Makes 10

Carbohydrate 13g each

1 Make the Frozen Berry Yogurt recipe up to the end of Step 2.
2 Divide the mixture among 10 x ¹/₃ cup posicle molds. Tap the molds on the counter to settle the mixture. Insert ice-block sticks and freeze for 4 hours or until set.
3 To serve, dip the molds into hot water for 5–10 seconds, then gently ease the popsicles out of the molds by pulling on the sticks. Serve immediately.

Mango frozen yogurt
Carbohydrate 25g per serving

9oz chopped frozen mango

Replace the frozen berries with the mango and make following the method above.

Custard bread pudding

Serves 4 Preparation time: 15 minutes Standing time: 15 minutes Cooking time: 25–30 minutes
Vegetarian Carbohydrate 70g per adult serving, 35g per child serving (excluding ice cream)

You can use sourdough instead of fruit bread if you prefer (or if that's what you have in the pantry).
Sprinkle $1/2$ cup raisins or currants between the bread pieces before adding the custard mixture.

$10^{1}/2$oz (about 6 thick slices) fruit or
   raisin loaf, crusts removed, lightly
   toasted
$1^{1}/2$oz pure fruit apricot spread
1 egg
6fl oz can light evaporated milk
4 tsp brown sugar
$1/2$ tsp vanilla essence
powdered sugar, to dust (optional)
light vanilla ice cream, to serve

1 Preheat oven to 350°F.
2 Spread 1 side of each toasted bread slice with the fruit spread and then cut into 1in pieces. Place the bread pieces in a 3 cup ovenproof dish and press down firmly.
3 Use a fork to whisk together the egg, evaporated milk, sugar and vanilla essence. Pour evenly over the bread in the dish. Set aside, pressing the bread down occasionally, for 15 minutes or until the bread has absorbed most of the liquid.
4 Place the dish in a deep roasting pan and add enough boiling water to the pan to reach halfway up the sides of the dish. Bake for 25–30 minutes or until the top is golden and the custard mixture is just set. Serve in scoops, sprinkled with powdered sugar (if using) and accompanied by vanilla ice cream.

VARIATION
Individual custard bread puddings
Carbohydrate 52g per serving (excluding ice cream)

Divide the Custard Bread Pudding mixture between 4 x $1/2$ cup ramekins and cook in the same way at 375°F for 20 minutes.

Dried fruit pillows

Makes 28 Preparation time: 20 minutes Standing time: 10 minutes Cooking time: 15 minutes
Vegetarian Carbohydrate 16g per cookie

These tempting sweet treats remind you why home-baked cookies are so much better than bought!
They are great for the lunch box or an after-school snack—though you may have to ration them out.

$3^1/_2$oz olive or canola oil margarine

$^1/_3$ cup Superfine sugar

1 tsp vanilla essence

1 egg

$1^3/_4$ cups plain flour

1 tsp baking soda

powdered sugar, to dust (optional)

FRUIT FILLING

$^1/_4$ cup unsweetened apple juice

1 cup pitted dates, coarsely
   chopped

$^1/_2$ cup raisins

$^1/_2$ tsp ground cinnamon

Cook's tip
These cookies will keep for up
to 1 week in an airtight
container at room temperature.

1 Process the margarine, sugar and vanilla essence in a food processor until combined. Add the egg and process until just combined. Sift flour and baking soda together. Add to the margarine mixture and combine using the pulse button, scraping down the sides of the bowl when necessary, until just combined. Turn onto a lightly floured surface and knead 3–4 times until dough is smooth. Divide the dough into 2 equal portions. Wrap in plastic wrap and place in the refrigerator while making the filling.
2 To make the filling, bring the apple juice to the boil in a small saucepan. Combine the dates, raisins and cinnamon in a heatproof bowl. Add the hot apple juice and set aside for 10 minutes. Transfer the fruit mixture to a food processor and process until almost smooth. Transfer to a bowl.
3 Preheat oven to 400°F and line a large baking tray with parchment paper.
4 Roll out 1 portion of the dough on a lightly floured surface with a lightly floured rolling pin to a 6 x 12in rectangle. Spread half the fruit filling over one half of the dough (down the long side), leaving a $^1/_2$in border around the edge. Fold the other half of the dough over the filling to cover and press the edges together to seal. Cut into $^3/_4$in wide fingers. Put the cookies on the lined tray and place uncovered in the refrigerator while repeating the process with the remaining portion of dough and filling.
5 Bake for 15 minutes or until lightly golden and cooked through. Cool on tray. Serve dusted with powdered sugar (if using).

Chocolate chip oat cookies

Makes 30 Preparation time: 15 minutes Cooking time: 15 minutes (per batch)
Vegetarian Carbohydrate 14g per cookie

Although we aim to develop recipes that have as low a GI as possible, there are some baked goods made with flour—like muffins and cookies—for which even we find this difficult. In this recipe we have replaced some of the margarine and flour with cannellini beans and rolled oats to help keep the GI (and fat) down. So enjoy them as an occasional treat. Use a good-quality dark chocolate, too. These aren't as crisp as traditional chocolate chip cookies, but just as delicious.

$^1/_3$ cup canned cannellini beans,
   drained and rinsed
1 egg
$2^1/_2$oz olive or canola oil margarine
$^3/_4$ cup firmly packed brown sugar
1 tsp vanilla essence
$5^1/_4$oz good-quality dark chocolate,
   chopped
$1^1/_3$ cups rolled oats
$^3/_4$ cup plain flour
$^1/_2$ tsp baking soda

1 Preheat oven to 375°F and line a large oven tray with parchment paper.
2 Use a small food processor or stick blender to puree the cannellini beans with the egg until smooth. Set aside.
3 Use electric beaters to beat the margarine, sugar and vanilla essence until smooth. Add the cannellini bean and egg mixture and beat until well combined.
4 Add the chocolate and rolled oats to the mixture and use a wooden spoon to stir in. Sift together the flour and baking soda over the biscuit mixture and stir until well combined.
5 Place heaped teaspoonfuls of the biscuit mixture onto the lined tray, about 2in apart (you will only use about half the mixture at this stage). Use your fingers to flatten each slightly. Bake for 15 minutes or until lightly golden around the edges and cooked through. Transfer to a wire rack to cook completely. Repeat with remaining mixture to make 30 cookies in total.

Cook's tip
These cookies will keep for up to 1 week in an airtight container at room temperature, but they will soften slightly.

Cinnamon, polenta and blueberry loaf

Makes 12 slices Preparation time: 15 minutes Cooking time: 50 minutes Cooling time: 5 minutes
Vegetarian, gluten-free and dairy-free Carbohydrate 34g per slice

This gluten- and dairy-free loaf will be popular as an after-school or lunch box treat. Try a slice toasted and topped with sliced banana and a drizzle of pure floral honey or maple syrup.

canola oil cooking spray
1 cup maize flour (polenta flour), sifted
4 tsp gluten-free baking powder
2 tsp ground cinnamon
$1^{1}/2$ cups fine polenta (cornmeal)
$^{1}/2$ cup firmly packed brown sugar
$1^{1}/4$ cups soy milk
$5^{1}/4$oz good-quality milk-free polyunsaturated or monounsaturated margarine, melted and cooled
1 egg, lightly whisked
2 egg whites
7oz fresh or thawed frozen blueberries

1 Preheat oven to 350°F. Spray a 4 x $8^{1}/2$in loaf pan with canola oil to lightly grease and line the base and two long sides with one piece of parchment paper.
2 Sift the maize flour, baking powder and cinnamon into a large bowl. Stir in the polenta and sugar and make a well in the center.
3 Use a fork to whisk together the soy milk, margarine, egg and egg whites in a medium-sized bowl until combined. Stir in the blueberries. Add to the dry ingredients and stir with a large metal spoon until just combined.
4 Spoon the mixture into the prepared pan and bake for 50 minutes or until a skewer inserted into the center comes out clean. Stand in pan for 5 minutes before turning onto a wire rack to cool. Serve cut into slices.

VARIATION
Cinnamon, polenta and blueberry muffins

Makes 12 slices Preparation time: 15 minutes Cooking time: 25 minutes Cooling time: 5 minutes
Vegetarian, gluten-free and dairy-free Carbohydrate 34g per muffin
You can also cook the muffins in 4 x 12-hole mini (1 tablespoon) non-stick muffin pans at 400°F for 15 minutes.
1 Lightly spray a 12-hole, $^{1}/3$ cup non-stick muffin pan with olive oil spray to grease.
2 Make using the same ingredients and method as above and up to the end of Step 3. Spoon the prepared mixture into the muffin pan and bake at 400°F for 25 minutes or until golden and cooked when tested with a skewer.

Cook's tips
- Store in an airtight container at room temperature for up to 2 days.
- To freeze the loaf or muffins, wrap individual slices or muffins in plastic wrap and then seal in a freezer bag or airtight container before freezing. Alternatively, pack in an airtight container and interleave with freezer wrap or parchment paper. Thaw at room temperature or toast the slices straight from the freezer.

Shopping tip
You can buy maize flour in health food shops, organic stores and larger supermarkets.

Chocolate hedgehog slice

Makes about 36 pieces Preparation time: 15 minutes Chilling time: 1–2 hours
Vegetarian Carbohydrate 11g per piece

These little sweets are a bit of a treat for special occasions, but if you give each child one on a plate with some fresh fruit alongside, you'll have a delightful mid-morning snack.

4^1/$_2$oz shredded whole-wheat cookies, broken into pieces

^{1}/$_2$ cup toasted walnuts or pecans, coarsely chopped

^{1}/$_2$ cup seedless raisins

9oz good-quality dark chocolate, chopped

2^1/$_4$oz olive or canola oil margarine

^{1}/$_4$ cup pure floral honey

powdered sugar, to dust (optional)

1 Line the base and 2 sides of a non-stick shallow 8in square pan with 1 piece of parchment paper.

2 Combine the shredded wheat cookies, walnuts and raisins in a medium-sized bowl.

3 Combine the chocolate, margarine and honey in a small saucepan and stir over low heat until chocolate has melted and ingredients are combined. Add to the biscuit mixture and stir with a wooden spoon to coat and combine evenly. Spoon mixture into the prepared pan and use the back of the spoon to smooth the surface.

4 Place slice in the refrigerator for 1–2 hours or until firm. Use the parchment paper to lift the slice from the pan. Cut into 1^1/$_4$in squares. Serve dusted with powdered sugar (if desired).

Cook's tip
Store in an airtight container in the refrigerator for up to 1 month.

basics

"The accompaniments that can make all the difference"

Cauliflower and broccoli bake

Serves 6 Preparation time: 15 minutes Cooking time: 25–30 minutes
Vegetarian Carbohydrate 10g per serving

Broccoli and cauliflower are part of the cruciferous vegetable family, which includes kale, cabbage, brussel sprouts and various Asian greens. They are in the vegetable superfood league being packed with vitamins, fiber, betacarotene, minerals and some iron and calcium for good measure. With their slightly bitter taste they aren't always popular with children, hence calling on the help of a cheesy sauce in a bake like this.

$1/2$ cauliflower (about 14oz)
1 head broccoli (about $10^1/_2$oz)
1 quantity Cheese Sauce (see recipe page 172)
2 tbsp reduced fat milk
1 cup firmly packed breadcrumbs (from day-old multigrain or sourdough bread)
$1/4$ cup finely grated parmesan
olive oil cooking spray

1 Preheat oven to 400°F.
2 Cut the cauliflower and broccoli into florets. Simmer in a medium-sized saucepan of boiling water for 3–5 minutes or until the vegetables are tender-crisp. (Be careful not to overcook at this stage.) Drain well.
3 Meanwhile, place the Cheese Sauce and milk in a small saucepan and heat over medium heat, stirring frequently, until just simmering.
4 Place the vegetables in a 6 cup ovenproof dish. Pour over the hot Cheese Sauce. Combine the breadcrumbs and parmesan and sprinkle over the vegetables. Spray the breadcrumb topping with a little olive oil.
5 Bake for 20–25 minutes or until the topping is golden. Serve immediately.

Cook's tip
You can prepare this bake a day ahead up to Step 4 then cover with plastic wrap and store in the refrigerator. Uncover and bake for 25–30 minutes.

Corn cakes

Serves 4 (makes 12) Preparation time: 10 minutes Cooking time: 8 minutes
Vegetarian Carbohydrate 5g per corn cake

These corn cakes also make a great snack when served with Guacamole (see recipe page 169). You will need about 1 cup fresh corn kernels for this recipe which can be replaced with the same amount of frozen corn kernels, thawed.

1 large corn cob, kernels removed
3 spring (green) onions, finely sliced
2 tbsp chopped flat-leaf (Italian) parsley or cilantro leaves (optional)
1 egg
$1/4$ cup plain flour, sifted
$1/4$ tsp baking powder
freshly ground black pepper, to taste (optional)
1 tsp olive oil

1 Place half the corn kernels with the spring onions, parsley or cilantro, egg, flour, baking powder and pepper (if using) in a food processor and process until well combined. Transfer to a medium-sized bowl and stir in the remaining corn kernels.
2 Heat $1/2$ teaspoon of the oil in a non-stick frying pan over medium heat and swirl to coat surface. Add small spoonfuls of the mixture to make 6 corn cakes and flatten slightly to about $1^{1}/_{2}$in in diameter. Cook for 2 minutes each side or until golden and cooked through. Transfer to a plate, set aside and keep warm. Repeat with the remaining oil and corn mixture to make 12 Corn Cakes in total. Serve warm.

Cook's tip

You can make the Corn Cakes a day ahead and store in an airtight container in the refrigerator. Reheat in a non-stick frying pan over medium heat for 2 minutes each side or until heated through.

Cheesy vegetable patties

Serves 6 (makes 12) Preparation time: 15 minutes (+ chilling time) Cooking time: 30 minutes
Vegetarian Carbohydrate 10g per patty

Sweet potatoes make a great substitute for potatoes and, like pumpkin, you can use them in sweet dishes, too. They are rich in nutrients including betacarotene, vitamin C and fiber, plus vitamin E, thiamin and folate. You can use this patty as a vegetable accompaniment or for a light meal or snack.

10¹/₂oz orange sweet potato (about 1 small)

¹/₂ x 14oz can cannellini beans, drained and rinsed

1 cup small broccoli florets

¹/₂ cup frozen peas

¹/₂ cup fresh or frozen corn kernels (see Cook's Tips below)

1 cup coarsely grated reduced fat cheddar cheese

1 egg yolk

1 tsp ground cumin

freshly ground black pepper, to taste (optional)

1¹/₂ cups firmly packed breadcrumbs (from day-old sourdough or multigrain bread)

2 tsp olive or canola oil

1 Peel the sweet potato. Halve lengthways and then cut into ¹/₂in thick slices. Place in a medium saucepan and cover with plenty of cold water. Bring to a boil over high heat. Boil gently for 15 minutes or until the sweet potato is very tender when tested with a fork or skewer. Drain well. Return to the saucepan, add the cannellini beans and use a potato masher to mash until smooth.

2 Meanwhile, add the broccoli, peas and corn to a saucepan of boiling water and cook for 1–2 minutes or until the peas and broccoli are bright green and tender-crisp. Drain well.

3 Add the broccoli, peas, corn, cheese, egg yolk and cumin to the mashed sweet potato and bean mixture and use a wooden spoon to combine evenly. Taste and season with pepper if desired. Cover the mixture and place in the refrigerator until cooled to room temperature.

4 Shape heaped tablespoonfuls of mixture into 12 patties about 2¹/₄in in diameter. Place the breadcrumbs on a plate and coat the patties with the crumbs, pressing on firmly.

5 Heat 1 teaspoon of the oil in a large non-stick frying pan over medium heat and swirl to coat the surface. Add half the patties to the pan and cook over medium heat for 2–3 minutes each side or until golden brown and heated through. Transfer to a plate, set aside and keep warm. Repeat with the remaining oil and patties. Serve warm.

Cook's tips
- You will need 1 small corn cob for this recipe if using fresh corn.
- As you only use half a can of beans, keep the leftovers for up to 2 days in an airtight container in the refrigerator to add to other recipes.
- Make the patties a day ahead and store in an airtight container in the refrigerator. Reheat in a non-stick frying pan over medium heat for 2 minutes each side or until heated through.

Hummus

Serves 6 (makes about 1 1/4 cups) Preparation time: 10 minutes
Vegetarian and gluten-free Carbohydrate 6g per serving

Made from chickpeas (garbanzo beans), Hummus has all the nutritional benefits of legumes including a low GI. Keep a tub on hand in the refrigerator as it is so versatile. You can use it as a dip for finger food snacks, as part of a sampling platter, or as a spread for sandwiches, rolls and wraps.

14oz canned chickpeas, drained
  and rinsed
4 tsp tahini paste (optional)
4 tsp olive oil
2 tbsp water
1 garlic clove
1/2 tsp ground cumin
1/4 tsp paprika (optional)
1 lemon, juiced
freshly ground black pepper,
  to taste

Place the chickpeas, tahini paste (if using), olive oil, water, garlic, cumin and paprika (if using) in a food processor and blend until well combined. Add lemon juice to taste and process until smooth. Add enough extra water to reach desired consistency. Taste and season with pepper.

Cook's tip
Store in a sealed airtight container in the refrigerator for up to a week.

Guacamole

Serves 4 Preparation time: 10 minutes
Vegetarian and gluten-free Carbohydrate 1g per serving

Packed with the good fats, this dip-accompaniment is best eaten straightaway, so make a smaller amount, and make it fresh each time. It only takes 10 minutes.

1 ripe medium avocado
2 tsp lime juice, or to taste
1 garlic clove, crushed
1 spring (green) onion, finely sliced
freshly ground black pepper
pinch salt (optional)
1 small ripe tomato, diced
1 tbsp chopped flat-leaf (Italian)
  parsley or cilantro leaves
  (optional)

Use a fork to mash the avocado flesh (make it as rough or smooth as you like). Add the lime juice, garlic and spring onion and stir until evenly combined. Taste and season with pepper, salt (if using) and/or a little more lime juice. Add the tomato and parsley or cilantro (if using) and stir gently to combine.

Sweet potato mash

Serves 4 Preparation time: 10 minutes Cooking time: 15 minutes
Vegetarian and gluten-free Carbohydrate 23g per adult serving, 12 g per child serving

For a change of flavor, try this using the same amount of freshly squeezed orange juice instead of the milk.

$10^{1}/_2$oz orange sweet potato (about 1 small)

$^{1}/_2$ x 14oz can cannellini beans, drained and rinsed

2 tsp olive oil margarine

2 tbsp reduced fat milk

1 tsp pure floral honey (optional)

freshly ground black pepper, to taste (optional)

1 Peel the sweet potato. Halve lengthways and then cut into $^{1}/_2$in thick slices. Place in a medium saucepan and cover with plenty of cold water. Bring to a boil over high heat. Boil gently for 15 minutes or until the sweet potato is very tender when tested with a fork or skewer. Drain well.

2 Return the hot sweet potato to the saucepan, add the cannellini beans and margarine and mash until smooth. Add the milk and honey (if using) and use a wooden spoon to beat until well combined and smooth. Taste and season with pepper (if using). Return to a low heat and stir until warmed through. Serve immediately.

Cook's tips

- As you only use half a can of beans, keep the leftovers for up to 2 days in an airtight container in the refrigerator to add to other recipes.
- You can make this mash a day ahead and store in an airtight container in the refrigerator. Reheat in a saucepan over medium heat, stirring frequently, until heated through. You may need to add a little water to reach desired consistency.

VARIATION
Squash mash

Carbohydrate 15g per adult serving, 7g per child serving

$10^{1}/_2$oz butternut squash, peeled, deseeded, cut into $^{3}/_4$in chunks

Replace the sweet potato with the squash, reduce the amount of milk to 1 tablespoon and follow the method above.

Roast vegetables

Serves 6 Preparation time: 10 minutes Cooking time: 1 hour
Vegetarian and gluten-free Carbohydrate 35g per adult serving

Some of these popular root vegetables have a high GI but, apart from sweet potato, they aren't rich sources of carbohydrate. They are, however, packed with vitamins, antioxidants and fiber, and simply scrumptious roasted this way as a side dish. What matters is that you eat a wide variety of nutritious foods. Enjoy a moderate portion with a dollop of Hummus to reduce the overall GI.

1 medium orange sweet potato
(about 17$\frac{1}{2}$oz)

2 medium parsnips (about 14oz)

2 medium carrots (about 9oz)

$\frac{1}{2}$ medium butternut squash
(about 24$\frac{1}{2}$oz)

3 tsp olive oil

pinch of salt

freshly ground black pepper,
to taste

4 sprigs rosemary, thyme or
oregano, leaves removed from
stems (optional)

1 quantity Hummus (see recipe
page 169), to serve

1 Preheat oven to 400°F and line a roasting pan with parchment paper.

2 Peel all the vegetables, deseed the squash and cut the vegetables into 1in chunks. Place them in the lined roasting pan, drizzle with the olive oil and sprinkle with salt, pepper and herbs (if using). Use your hands to toss the vegetables to coat with the oil and seasonings.

3 Bake for 1 hour, or until golden and tender, tossing the vegetables about 3 times during cooking. Serve immediately with the Hummus.

Cheese sauce

Serves 4 (makes about 1 cup) Preparation time: 5 minutes Cooking time: 10 minutes
Vegetarian Carbohydrate 6g per 1/4 cup serving

3 tsp olive oil margarine

4 tsp plain flour

1 cup reduced fat milk

1/2 cup coarsely grated reduced fat
   cheddar cheese

1/4 tsp Dijon mustard

freshly ground black pepper,
   to taste (optional)

1 Melt the margarine in a small saucepan over medium heat. Stir in the flour and cook, stirring, for 2 minutes.

2 Remove saucepan from heat and use a small balloon whisk to gradually whisk in the milk until combined and smooth. Return the saucepan to a medium–low heat and stir with the whisk until thickened and simmering. Cook, stirring, for a further minute. (If the sauce is still a little lumpy, don't worry—simply strain it through a sieve.)

3 Remove the sauce from the heat. Add the cheese and mustard and stir until the cheese melts. Taste and season with pepper, if desired.

Cook's tip

To store, place in an airtight container and cover the surface of the sauce directly with plastic wrap. Seal the container and keep in the refrigerator for up to 2 days.

Easy tomato sauce

Serves 4–6 (makes about 2 cups) Preparation time: 5 minutes Cooking time: 35–40 minutes
Vegetarian and Gluten-free Carbohydrate 10g per ½ cup serving

2 tsp olive oil
1 brown onion, finely chopped
2 garlic cloves, crushed
2 x 14oz cans no-added-salt diced
    tomatoes and juice
2 tbsp no-added-salt tomato paste
1 tsp sugar, or to taste
freshly ground black pepper,
    to taste

1 Combine the olive oil and onion in a medium-sized saucepan and cook, stirring occasionally, over medium heat for 5–8 minutes or until onion is soft. Add the garlic and cook for a further minute.
2 Add the tomatoes, their juice, and the tomato paste, and bring to a simmer. Reduce heat to low–medium and cook, uncovered and stirring occasionally, for 25–30 minutes or until thickened to a good sauce consistency. Taste and season with sugar and pepper.

Cook's tip
Store in an airtight container in the refrigerator for up to 3 days. Or freeze in a labeled airtight container for up to 2 months. Thaw in the refrigerator overnight.

pantry revamp

Healthy eating isn't an accident. It's only going to happen with planning and preparation. Rethinking how you shop, store and prepare food can improve the whole household's eating habits. Here are some tips to make preparing healthy meals easier.

Your checkout choices: the healthy home shopping list

Here is a practical shopping list to stock your fridge, pantry and freezer.

First, plan a day when you remove all the "junk" foods you normally keep in your pantry—the cakes, cookies, snacks, chocolates, sweetened drinks and so on. Go shopping in the afternoon (don't go hungry!) for healthy substitutes, as suggested in the following list.

What to keep in your pantry

Asian sauces—chili, hoi sin, oyster, soy and fish sauces are a good basic range. Look for salt-reduced versions.

Barley—one of the oldest cultivated cereals, barley is very nutritious and high in soluble fiber. Look for products such as pearl barley to use in soups, stews and pilafs.

Black pepper—buy ground pepper or grind your own peppercorns.

Bread—low GI options include grainy, soy and flaxseed, stoneground whole-grain, pumpernickel, sourdough, English muffins, low GI white, flat bread and pita bread.

Breakfast cereals—including traditional rolled oats, natural muesli and low GI packaged breakfast cereals.

Bulgur wheat—use it to make tabbouleh, or add to vegetable burgers, stuffings, soups and stews.

Canned evaporated skim milk—this is an excellent substitute for cream in pasta sauces.

Canned fish—keep a good stock of canned tuna packed in springwater, and canned sardines and salmon.

Canned fruit—have a variety on hand, including peaches, pears, apples and nectarines—choose the brands labeled "no added sugar" or "in natural juice."

Canned vegetables—sweet corn kernels and tomatoes can help boost the vegetable content of a meal.

Couscous—ready in minutes; serve with casseroles and braised dishes.

Curry pastes—a tablespoon or so makes a delicious curry base.

Dried fruit—such as apricots, raisins, prunes and apples.

Dried herbs—oregano, basil, ground cilantro, thyme and rosemary can be very useful, not to mention convenient.

Honey—try to avoid the commercial honeys or honey blends and use "pure floral" honeys, which have a much lower GI; these include yellow-box and red gum.

Jam—a dollop of good-quality jam or fruit spread (with no added sugar) on toast has fewer calories than butter or margarine.

Legumes—stock a variety of legumes (dried or canned), including lentils, chickpeas, split peas and beans; there are many bean varieties, including cannellini, butter, borlotti, kidney and soybeans.

Mustard—seeded or whole-grain mustard is useful as a sandwich spread, and in salad dressings and sauces.

Noodles—many Asian noodles, such as hokkien, udon and rice vermicelli, are low to medium GI because of their dense texture, whether they are made from wheat or rice flour.

Nuts—try them sprinkled over your breakfast cereal, salad or dessert; try unsalted nuts as a snack as well.

Oils—try olive oil for general use; extra virgin olive oil for salad dressings and marinades; sesame oil for Asian-style stir-fries; and canola or olive oil cooking sprays.

Pasta—a great source of carbohydrates and B vitamins. Fresh or dried, the preparation is easy: cook in boiling water until just tender (al dente), then drain and top with your favorite sauce (not made with cream) or stir through plenty of vegetables and a sprinkle of parmesan cheese.

Quinoa—this whole grain cooks in 10–15 minutes and has a slightly chewy texture. It can be used as a substitute for pasta, rice, couscous or bulgur. Note: it is important to rinse the grains thoroughly before cooking.

Rice—Basmati or Japanese sushi rice (Koshihikari) varieties are good choices because they have a lower GI than, for example, jasmine rice.

Rolled oats—besides making oatmeal, oats can be added to cakes, cookies, breads and desserts.

Spices—most spices, including ground cumin, turmeric, cinnamon, paprika and nutmeg, should be bought in small quantities because they lose pungency with age and incorrect storage. A really useful Web site to find out all about how to use dried herbs and spices in your cooking is www.mccormick.com

Stock—make your own stock or buy long-life ready-made products; to keep the sodium content down with ready-made stocks, look out for salt-reduced ones.

Tomato paste—use in soups, sauces and casseroles. Buy no-added-salt varieties.

Vinegar—white wine, red wine and balsamic vinegars are excellent bases for vinaigrette dressings in salads.

What to keep in your refrigerator

Bottled vegetables—sun-dried tomatoes, olives, roasted eggplant and pepper are flavorsome additions to pastas and sandwiches.

Capers, olives and anchovies—these can be bought in jars and kept in the refrigerator once opened. They are a tasty addition to pasta dishes, salads and pizzas. Use sparingly.

Cheese—any reduced fat cheese is great. A block of parmesan is indispensable and will keep for up to a month. Reduced fat cottage and ricotta cheeses have a short life so are best bought as needed; they can be a good alternative to butter or margarine in a sandwich.

Condiments—jars of minced garlic, chili or ginger are convenient and will spice up your cooking in an instant.

Eggs—to increase your intake of omega-3 fats, we suggest using omega-3-enriched eggs. Although the yolk is high in cholesterol, the fat in eggs is predominantly monounsaturated, and therefore considered a "good fat."

Fish—try a variety of fresh fish.

Fresh fruit—almost all fruit makes an excellent snack. Try apples, oranges, pears, grapes, grapefruit, peaches, apricots, strawberries and mangoes.

Fresh herbs—these are available in most supermarkets and there really is no substitute for their flavor. For variety, try parsley, basil, mint, chives and cilantro.

Meat—try lean beef, lamb fillets, pork fillets, chicken (breast, lean thighs or drumsticks) and ground beef.

Milk—skim or low fat milk is best, or low fat calcium-enriched soy milk.

Vegetables—keep seasonal vegetables on hand, such as spinach, broccoli, cauliflower, Asian greens, asparagus and zucchini. Pepper, spring (green) onions and mung bean and snow pea sprouts are great for salads. Sweet corn and sweet potato are essential to your low GI food store.

Yogurt—low fat plain yogurt gives you the most calcium for the fewest calories. Have vanilla or fruit versions as a dessert, or use plain yogurt as a condiment in savory dishes. If using yogurt in a hot meal, make sure you add it at the last minute, and do not let it boil.

What to keep in your freezer

Frozen berries—berries can make any dessert special, and frozen berries mean you don't have to wait until berry season. Blueberries, raspberries and strawberries are a fantastic source of antioxidants and vitamin C.

Frozen vegetables—keep a packet of peas, beans, corn, spinach or mixed vegetables in the freezer; these are always handy to add to a quick meal.

Frozen yogurt—this is a fantastic substitute for ice cream and some products even have a similar creamy texture, but with much less fat.

Ice cream—reduced or low fat ice cream is ideal for a quick dessert, served with fresh fruit.

Directory

ALLERGY
American Academy of Allergy, Asthma & Immunology
www.aaaai.org

The Food Allergy & Anaphylaxis Network
www.foodallergy.org

CELIAC DISEASE
Celiac Disease Foundation
www.celiac.org

DIABETES
American Diabetes Association (ADA)
www.diabetes.org

Canadian Diabetes Association
www.diabetes.ca

Juvenile Diabetes Research Foundation International
www.jdrf.org and click on "Locations"

FIND A DIETITIAN
American Dietetic Association
www.eatright.org

Dietitians of Canada
www.dieticians.ca

FOOD ADDITIVES
Food and Drug Administration
www.fda.gov

GLYCEMIC INDEX
University of Sydney Glycemic Index Database
www.glycemicindex.com

HEALTH
Health Canada
www.hc-sc.gc.ca

KidsHealth
www.kidshealth.org

U.S. Department of Health & Human Services
www.healthfinder.gov

NUTRITION
American Dietetic Association
www.eatright.org

Nutrition.gov
www.nutrition.gov

PARENTING
Parenting Help
www.parenting.org

Acknowledgments

The real stars of this book are the children. Not only did they eat everything put in front of them (including their greens), they were an absolute pleasure to work with. So a very big thank you to April and Rowan, Brandon and Kaitlin, Brooke and Ben, Catherine and Cassie, Charlotte and Fergus, Declan and Liam, Hana and Poppy, and Pia and Sophie. We hope you had fun and that you meant it when you said the food was yummy. And thank you also to their parents who waited patiently on the sidelines!

Food photography is something of an art form these days. But we didn't want art form images, we wanted real food in the right proportions on the plate—just how a healthy meal for the family should look if you cooked it at home yourself. So, to our photographer, Ian Hofstetter, and stylist, Katy Holder, a huge, huge thank you for listening to our ideas and then bringing yours to the table to make our family fare look so delicious.

The nuts and bolts of putting books together happens inside publishing companies. What you see in front of you may look effortless, but we know how much thought, imagination and attention to detail the Hachette Livre Australia team have put into this. We would like to thank one and all for their support and encouragement, especially our editors Simone Ford and Jacquie Brown, and "nothing's too much trouble to do again" designer Judi Rowe. As for production editor Anna Waddington, thank you for finding the extra days so cheerfully when we needed them.

As ever we are indebted to the seemingly tireless Fiona Hazard, Publishing Director at Hachette Livre Australia, and Matthew Lore, Vice President and Executive Editor at Da Capo Lifelong Books. We want you to know how much we appreciate your ongoing support, and that we do understand that without you books like this just wouldn't happen.

One very special person held on to the vision for this book and made it a reality—Vanessa Radnidge, our publisher. Thank you.

Index

A

activity 26
  activity pyramid 27
  fluids 29
  fueling active kids 28
  sport 29
allergies 30–1
almond cereal, gluten-free 68
apples 39
  apple and mixed berry juice 82
  apple and pear crumble
    with maple syrup yogurt 150
apricot smoothie 90

B

baked beans 39
  toasted sandwich 109
baked crispy fish pieces 116
bananas
  banana bread 77
  banana porridge 58
  banana smoothie 66
barbecued satay lamb kebabs
  130
beef
  beef and lentil burgers 109
  beef stir-fry with noodles,
    corn and snow peas 139
berry yogurt, frozen 154
beverages 22–3
breads and cereals 39
  almond cereal, gluten-free 68
  crunchy homemade cereal 61
  doughnuts, cookies, crackers
    and cakes 14
  gluten-free 33
  high fiber 14
  low GI, with 14
  oats 33
  recommended daily intake 15
breakfast
  banana smoothie 66
  couscous 57

fried rice 69
breakfasts and brunches 54–71

C

calcium, non-dairy sources 18
canned fruit 39, 90
carbohydrates per serving 52
carrot, apple and celery juice 82
cauliflower and broccoli bake
  166
cereal, crunchy homemade 61
cheese sauce 172
cheesy vegetable patties 168
chicken
  chicken and pumpkin soup
    with quinoa 124
  chicken curry with chickpeas,
    squash and spinach 112
  chicken sang choy bau 140
  creamy chicken and corn
    soup 106
  soy and sesame marinated
    chicken drumsticks 122
  Thai chicken meatballs 123
chickpea, squash and
  spinach curry 112
children
  activity 26–9
  bread and cereals 14–15
  dairy foods 18–19
  drinking requirements 22–3
  fat intake 21
  fluid intake 22–3
  food allergies and
    intolerances 30–1
  fruit 10–11
  fussy eaters 36–7
  guidelines for healthy eating 4
  healthy weight, what is 35
  hunger and 38–9
  lactose intolerance 31
  mealtimes and 9
  menu plans see menu plans
    for children
  nutritional needs 8

overweight 34
protein 16–17
raising food-smart kids
refusal to drink milk 18
refusal to eat meat 17
sport 29
toddlers 11
too much milk, effect of 19
treats, fast food and
  takeout 24–5
underweight 35
vegetables 10, 12, 13
chocolate chip oat cookies 158
chocolate hedgehog slice 162
cinnamon, polenta and
  blueberry loaf/muffins 161
celiac disease 32–3
conversions,
  dry/temperature 52
cookies 14
  nutty oat cookies 86
cooking the low GI way 52
cordial 22
corn cakes 167
couscous, breakfast 57
creamy chicken and corn soup
  106
crunchy homemade cereal 61
custard bread pudding 156

D

dairy foods 18
  recommended daily intake 19
desserts and sweet treats
  148–63
dried fruit pillows 157
drinks 22–3

E

eggs 16
  easy egg ideas 71
  eggs in nests 65
  recommended daily intake 17
English muffin, fruity 90
exercise 26–9

F
fast food 24–5
fats and oils 20
  recommended daily intake 21
  saturated fats 20
  source of good fats 21
fiber in foods 15
fish 16
  baked crispy fish pieces 116
  benefits of 16
  mercury in 16
  pan-fried 115
  recommended daily intake
    17
fluid intake 22–3
  liquid calories 23
food allergies and intolerances
    30–1
  lactose intolerance 31
  preventing food allergy 31
foods for hungry children 39
freezer, what to keep in 178
French toast with strawberry
  and banana topping 62
fried rice
  breakfast 69
  easy 127
frittata, ham and vegetable
    96
frozen berry yogurt 154
fruit 10
  canned, ideas for 90
  fresh, frozen or canned 10
  juice 22
  recommended daily intake 11
  servings 11
fruit and nut muesli bars 89
fruit skewers with passion fruit
  yogurt dip 153
fruity dessert parfaits 90
fruity English muffin 90
full-of-fruit muffins 81

G
gluten-free foods 32–3
  gluten-free almond cereal 68

Glycemic Index (GI) 7
guacamole 169
guidelines for healthy eating 5

H
ham and vegetable frittata 96
healthy eating, guidelines for 5
high-fiber foods 15
hokkien noodles with pork,
  vegetable and egg 131
honey and oregano roasted
  leg of lamb with roasted
    vegetables 128
hummus 169
  tortilla wedges and vegetable
    sticks, with 74

I
ice cream 39
iron 19
Italian meatballs with spaghetti
  136

J
juices 82

L
lactose intolerance 31
lamb
  barbecued satay lamb kebabs
    130
  honey and oregano roasted
    leg of lamb with roasted
      vegetables 128
  lamb cutlets with spiced pilaf
    132
  lamb patties with bulgur 135
legumes 16
  easy ways with 109
  recommended daily intake 17
liquid calories 23
low GI eating
  advantages of 6
  cooking 52
  gluten-free 32
lunch-box basics 107
lunches 92–109

M
macaroni and cheese 120
main dishes 110–47
mango frozen yogurt 154
mango milkshake 84
mealtimes 9
measurements,
  dry/temperature 52
meat 16
  recommended daily intake
    17
meatballs in tomato sauce with
  couscous 136
menu plans for children 41
  preschool children 43
  school children 47
  teens 49
  young children 45
mercury in fish 16
milk 18, 19, 22, 39
muesli bars, fruit and nut 89
muffins
  fruity English 90
  full-of-fruit 81

N
noodles 39
nutty oat biscuits 86

O
oat pikelets 78
oats 33
  nutty oat biscuits 86
  pikelets 78
omelette, tomato, ham and
  cheese 71

P
pan-fried fish 115
pantry, what to keep in 176–7
pasta 39
  easy ideas 147
  Italian meatballs with
    spaghetti 136
  macaroni and cheese 120
  pasta with squash sauce 147

squash and spinach lasagna 144

spaghetti bolognese 144

speedy pasta with tomatoes and basil 147

tomato tuna pasta, easy 98

peach slushie 90

pear and mandarin juice 82

pearl barley risotto with squash and spinach 145

picky eaters 36–7

pikelets, oat 78

pineapple and passion fruit juice 82

popcorn, homemade 85

popsicles, frozen berry yoghurt 154

porridge 39

  banana 58

  quinoa, with pears and golden syrup 59

poultry 16

  recommended daily intake 17

preschool children

  7-day menu plan 43

Q

quiches, quick mini 71

quinoa porridge with pears and golden syrup 59

R

raisin banana bread 77

recipes

  carbohydrates per serving 52

  measures 52

  serving size 52

refrigerator, what to keep in 177–8

rice-paper rolls, vegetable 94

roasted vegetables, 171

roasted vegetables with chickpeas 109

S

salmon

salmon and pasta pie 101

salmon cakes with lemon sauce 119

sang choy bau 140

satay lamb kebabs, barbecued 130

saturated fats 20

school children

  7-day menu plan 47

scrambled egg, simple 71

seafood 16

  recommended daily intake 17

shopping list 176–8

snacks 72–91

soft drinks 22

soups

  chicken and pumpkin soup with quinoa 124

  creamy chicken and corn soup 106

  tomato and red lentil soup with toast fingers 104

  vegetable soup with beans 109

soy and sesame marinated chicken drumsticks 122

spaghetti bolognese 144

sports

  fluids 29

  requirements before, during and after 29

squash and spinach lasagna 144

sushi, tuna and cucumber 102–3

sweet corn 39

sweet potato mash 170

T

tacos, vegetarian 143

takeout 24–5

  healthier takeaout options 24–5

teens

  7-day menu plan 49

Thai chicken meatballs 123

toddlers 11

tomato

  tomato and red lentil soup with toast fingers 104

  tomato sauce, easy 173

  tomato tuna pasta, easy 98

treats 24–5

  size of 25

tuna

  tomato tuna pasta, easy 98

  tuna and cucumber sushi 102–3

  tuna cakes 118

  tuna pasta, speedy 147

  tuna rice bake 114

  tuna, tomato, cucumber and couscous salad 99

V

veal and pork sang choy bau 140

vegetable rice-paper rolls 94

vegetable soup with beans 109

vegetables 10, 12

  cooking tips 12

  recommended daily intake 13

  rice-paper rolls 94

  roasted, 171

  roasted, with chickpeas 109

vegetarian tacos 143

W

walnut banana bread 77

water 22

  bottled 22

watermelon, orange and mint juice 82

Web-sites 179

weight

  healthy, what is 35

  overweight children 34

  underweight children 35

Y

young children

  7-day menu plan 45

Text copyright © 2008 Jennie Brand-Miller, Kaye Foster-Powell, Philippa Sandall and Anneka Manning
Photography copyright © 2008 Hachette Livre Australia Pty Limited
Photography copyright © 2008 pp. viii, 9, 17, 21 Getty Images

This edition was published in somewhat different form in Australia by Hachette Livre Australia. This edition is published by arrangement with Hachette Livre Australia.

Cataloging-in-Publication data for this book is available from the Library of Congress.

First Da Capo Press edition 2008
ISBN-10 1-60094-033-1
ISBN-13 978-1-60094-033-0

Published by Da Capo Press
A Member of the Perseus Books Group
www.dacapopress.com

Note: The information in this book is true and complete to the best of our knowledge. This book is intended only as an informative guide for those wishing to know more about health issues. In no way is this book intended to replace, countermand, or conflict with the advice given to you by your own physician. The ultimate decision concerning care should be made between you and your doctor. We strongly recommend you follow his or her advice. Information in this book is general and is offered with no guarantees on the part of the authors of Da Capo Press. The authors and publisher disclaim all liability in connection with the use of this book.

Da Capo Press books are available at special discounts for bulk purchases in the United States by corporations, institutions, and other organizations. For more information, please contact the Special Markets Department at the Perseus Books Group, 2300 Chestnut Street, Suite 200, Philadelphia, PA 19103, or call (800) 255-1514, or e-mail special.markets@perseusbooks.com.

1 2 3 4 5 6 7 8 9—09 08 07 06

Photographer: Ian Hofstetter
Stylist: Katy Holder
Designer: Judi Rowe, Agave Creative Group
Editor: Simone Ford
Props courtesy of MUD Australia, Gina Cucina and Tupperware

Printed in China

NOTE

All recipes in this book use 4 tbsp eggs.

Liquid Measurements

1fl oz	2 tbsp	30ml
2fl oz	$1/4$ cup	60ml
$2^3/4$fl oz	$1/3$ cup	80ml
4fl oz	$1/2$ cup	125ml
6fl oz	$3/4$ cup	185ml
8fl oz	1 cup	250ml